Revise IB

World religions

TestPrep: DP Exam Practice Workbook

A note from us

While every effort has been made to provide accurate advice on the assessments for this subject, the only authoritative and definitive source of guidance and information is published in the official subject guide, teacher support materials, specimen papers and associated content published by the IB. Please refer to these documents in the first instance for advice and guidance on your assessments.

Any exam-style questions in this book have been written to help you practise and revise your knowledge and understanding of the content before your exam. Remember that the actual exam questions may not look like this.

Lead author: Andrea Skafish Beder

Contributing authors: Rachel Pitkin, Kariman Mango

SL
Standard Level

Published by Extend Education Ltd., Alma House, 73 Rodney Road, Cheltenham, UK GL50 1HT

www.extendeducation.com

The right of Andrea Skafish Beder, Rachel Pitkin and Kariman Mango to be identified as authors of this work has been asserted by them with the Copyright, Designs and Patents Act 1988.

Reviewed by Hesham Elnagar

Typesetting by York Publishing Solutions Pvt. Ltd., INDIA

Cover photo by Louis Maniquet on Unsplash

First published 2020

24 23 22 21 20

10 9 8 7 6 5 4 3 2 1

ISBN 978-1-913121-06-8

Author acknowledgements

Many thanks to the students at The Brooklyn Latin School.

Copyright notice

Other important information

A reminder that Extend Education is not in any way affiliated with the International Baccalaureate.

Many people have worked to create this book. We go through rigorous editorial processes, including separate answers checks and expert reviews of all content. However, we all make mistakes. So if you notice an error in the paper, please let us know at info@extendeducation.co.uk so we can make sure it is corrected at the earliest possible opportunity.

If you are an educator with a passion for creating content and would like to write for us, please contact info@extendeducation.co.uk or write to us through the contact form on our website www.extendeducation.co.uk.

CONTENTS

HOW TO USE THIS BOOK

This excellent exam practice book has been designed to help you prepare for your world religions exam. It is divided into three sections.

EXPLAIN

The EXPLAIN section gives you a rundown of your paper, including number of marks available, how much time you'll have and the assessment objectives (AOs) and command terms. There's also a handy checklist of your topics you can use as a revision checklist.

SHOW

The SHOW section gives you some examples of different questions you will come across in the exam. It's designed to help you learn the question types and the kinds of answers you need to give to get you the maximum number of marks.

TEST

This is your chance to try out what you've learned. The TEST section has full sets of exam-style practice papers filled with the same type and number of questions that you can expect to see in the exam. The first set of papers has got a lot of helpful tips and suggestions for answering the questions. The middle set has more general advice – make sure you have revised before testing yourself with this set. The last set has no help at all. Not one single hint! Make sure you do this one a bit closer to your exam to check what else you might need to revise.

Set A

Paper 1 & Paper 2

Presented with a lot of tips and guidance to help you to get to the correct answer and boost your confidence!

Use these papers early on in your revision.

Set B

Paper 1 & Paper 2

Presented with fewer helpful suggestions so you have to rely on your revision before trying these.

Test yourself using these papers when you are a bit more confident.

Set C

Paper 1 & Paper 2

Presented with space to add your own notes and no guidance - the perfect way to test whether you are exam ready.

Use these papers as close as you can to the exam.

All questions are presented with **ANSWERS** so you can check how you did in your practice papers.

Features

Take a look at some of the helpful features in these books that are designed to support you as you do your practice papers.

These will point you in the direction of the right answer!

These are general hints for answering the questions.

These are referred to as AOs all the way through this book

This box reminds you of the Assessment Objective being tested.

Beware of making the common and easy-to-avoid mistakes!

These flag up common or easy-to-make mistakes that might cost you marks.

The command terms are a clue to how you should answer the questions

COMMAND TERMS

These boxes outline what the command term is asking you to do.

For example, links to TOK or Extended Essay!

These show you when the questions have other interdisciplinary links.

These boxes contain really useful advice about what examiners are looking for

ANSWER ANALYSIS

These boxes include advice on how to get the most possible marks for your answer.

KNOWING YOUR PAPER

It is important to be familiar with the exam format for the world religions standard level (SL) exam to ensure that you feel confident and prepared on the day of the exam. The goals of the exams are to showcase your knowledge and understanding of the content and concepts from five of the major world religions and analyse them. Reviewing and revising the content and practising the types of questions will help you to feel prepared to take the world religions SL exams. Let's get started!

How are you assessed?

You will complete two written exams on different days for Diploma Programme (DP) world religions.

Paper 1	Paper 2
Candidates must answer **five** questions with at least one question from Sections A, B and C	Candidates must answer **two** questions with one from Section A and one from Section B
Short answer written responses	Essay responses
30% of overall grade	45% of overall grade
45 marks (9 marks per question)	30 marks (15 marks per question)
1 hour 15 minutes	1 hour 30 minutes

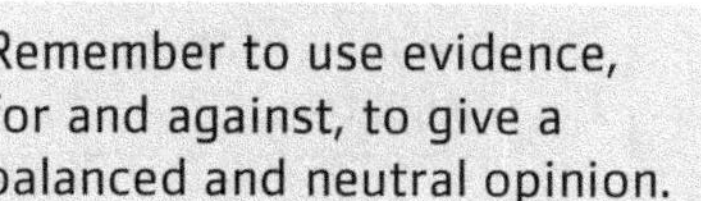

In your answers you cannot be biased or use stereotypes. They need to be from an outside perspective, rather than your own internal perspective.

Consider the diversity of ideas among and within religions.

ANSWER ANALYSIS

Remember to use evidence, for and against, to give a balanced and neutral opinion.

Remember that the goal of the DP world religions course is to promote empathy and respect for diverse religious traditions.

You will not have studied all the religions included in Sections A and B. Don't panic! Just choose the questions on the religions you have studied.

The last 25% of your grade will be based on your internal assessment (your religious investigation).

ANSWER ANALYSIS

Paper 1 – each question will have a short text related to a specific religion, followed by two short-answer questions (part (a) and part (b)). You will need to answer both parts.

Make sure you do not repeat the same idea for parts (a) and (b).

ANSWER ANALYSIS

Paper 2 – use a formal essay format:
- introductory paragraph with a thesis
- at least three body paragraphs
- and a conclusion that includes additional analysis of the topic.

Paper 1 – each mark represents a fully developed, independent idea that is clearly and simply written.

Paper 2 – in each section there will be six questions about specific religions and one open-ended question that can link back to many religions.

Your assessment objectives

There are **three** assessment objectives for DP world religions. Make sure that you are clear on what you are expected to demonstrate for each objective by referring to the table below.

Assessment objective	What questions use this?	Example question
Assessment objective 1: Knowledge and understanding	**Paper 1, Section A, B & C** Questions in the exam that test your understanding of AO1 are Paper 1, part (a) and these questions are worth 3 marks. You will be asked to show knowledge and understanding of specific content from a religion by responding to a question that follows a short text related to that religion.	**Question 1–9 (a):** Identify three teachings in this passage. **[3 marks]**
Assessment objective 2: Application and analysis	**Paper 1, Section A, B & C** Questions in the exam that test your understanding of AO2 are Paper 1, part (b) and these questions are worth 6 marks. You will be asked to show your understanding by applying your content knowledge as it relates to the text and to analyse how that information connects to key concepts in the religion.	**Question 1–9 (b):** Explain the significance of prayer in Islam. **[6 marks]**
Assessment objective 3: Synthesis and evaluation	**Paper 2, Section A, B & C** Questions in the exam that test your understanding of AO3 are Paper 2 questions and these questions are worth 15 marks. You will be asked to evaluate key concepts and synthesize evidence and analysis. Paper 2 questions test assessment objectives 1–4 by asking candidates to write in-depth essay responses that show knowledge (AO1), analysis (AO2), evaluation and synthesis (AO3), and appropriate skills (AO4).	**Questions 1–14:** Discuss the significance of ahimsa in Hinduism. **[15 marks]**
Assessment objective 4: Application of skills	Your Internal Assessment is heavily focused on AO4 and these skills transfer to your Paper 2 questions, which are worth 15 marks. AO4 requires that you use and apply skills that are appropriate to the demands of the question in order to write a clear, balanced, and logical account and that you consider the reliability of sources.	

COMMAND TERMS

Identify, outline, describe

COMMAND TERMS

Explain, analyse

COMMAND TERMS

Discuss, to what extent, compare, contrast, compare and contrast, examine, evaluate

Before you begin

The DP World Religions course covers a range of content with an academic and empathetic understanding of the diverse belief systems around the world. The study of religions enables you to understand the perspectives of religious practitioners and adherents and the ways that the practice of a religion may impact that person's and/or community's daily life and interactions with others.

The course includes an introductory unit, and a thorough exploration of five of the nine religions, an in-depth study of two of those five religions, and a final religious investigation, which is the internal assessment.

In order to perform your best on the external assessment (the Paper 1 and Paper 2 examinations), you should have a clear understanding of the content and concepts listed below.

Put a tick in the box when you feel confident that you could respond to each of the following prompts with specific vocabulary and detailed content.

Introduction to world religions

You should have enough knowledge of five religions from this list of nine in order to answer a Paper 1 question on each theme.

Religion	The human condition	Where we are going	How we get there
Hinduism	☐	☐	☐
Buddhism	☐	☐	☐
Sikhism	☐	☐	☐
Judaism	☐	☐	☐
Christianity	☐	☐	☐
Islam	☐	☐	☐
Taoism	☐	☐	☐
Jainism	☐	☐	☐
Baha'i Faith	☐	☐	☐

In-depth studies of world religions

You will study two of these religions in depth on the following themes for your Paper 2 exam.

Religion	Rituals	Sacred texts	Doctrines/ beliefs	Religious experience	Ethics and moral conduct
Hinduism	☐	☐	☐	☐	☐
Buddhism	☐	☐	☐	☐	☐
Sikhism	☐	☐	☐	☐	☐
Judaism	☐	☐	☐	☐	☐
Christianity	☐	☐	☐	☐	☐
Islam	☐	☐	☐	☐	☐

You should feel confident on the meaning of, and how to use, the following vocabulary in the context of the following religions.

Hinduism	
Ahimsa	☐
Ascetic	☐
Atman	☐
Brahman	☐
Darshan	☐
Dharma	☐
Karma	☐
Moksha	☐
Murti	☐
Samsara	☐
Trimurti	☐
Yoga	☐

Buddhism	
Anatta	☐
Bodhisatta/Bodhisattva	☐
Buddha	☐
Dhamma/Dharma	☐
Dukkha/Dukha	☐
Eightfold Path	☐
Four Noble Truths	☐
Kamma/Karma	☐
Nirvana	☐
Samsara	☐
Sangha	☐
Tanha/Trishna	☐

Sikhism	
Gromukh	☐
Gurprasad	☐
Gurus	☐
Haumai	☐
Jot	☐
Kirtan	☐
Manmukh	☐
Maya	☐
Mukti	☐
Nadar	☐
Nam japna	☐
Nirguna	☐

Judaism	
Abrahamic Covenant	☐
Chosen people	☐
Halakhah	☐
Israel	☐
Monotheism	☐
Mosaic Covenant	☐
Mitzvah	☐
Mitzvot	☐
Talmud	☐
Tikkun olam	☐
Torah	☐
Transcendent	☐

Christianity	
Agape	☐
Atonement	☐
Baptism	☐
Grace	☐
Jesus	☐
Kingdom of Heaven	☐
Original Sin	☐
Redemption	☐
Resurrection	☐
Sacraments	☐
Salvation	☐
Trinity	☐

Islam	
Akhirah	☐
Day of Judgement	☐
Five Pillars	☐
Halal and haram	☐
Iman	☐
Islam	☐
Jihad	☐
Monotheism	☐
Prophet Muhammad (PBUH)	☐
Risalah	☐
Tawhid	☐
Umma	☐

! Your exam is handwritten, and you must use a blue or black ink pen. You cannot use marker pen or pencil or any correctional fluid or tape.

! In your answers avoid personal religious connections and personal pronouns, and be aware of insider and outsider approaches.

When structuring your responses, consider the various movements, sects, or denominations within the religious tradition.

What to do in your exam

Get a good night's sleep the night before the exam. Do not try to prepare too much the night before.

Make sure that you have a blue or black ink pen (and a spare!)

During the 5-minute reading period before the start of each exam, read each question carefully. (You will not be able to use a pen during this time; it is only for reading.)

When the exam begins, note the questions you can answer and cross out the rest.

For Paper 1 exams, select the questions for the five religions that you studied in class. For Paper 2 exams, underline the key content that you know in each of the questions. The question with the most underlined content is a great place to start!

Once you've chosen your questions and have finished planning, take a deep breath and begin.

Time management can be a challenge, so try to spend approximately 15 minutes on each Paper 1 response and 45 minutes on each Paper 2 response.

Briefly write down any religious vocabulary, key content, and themes next to the questions.

ANSWER ANALYSIS

For Paper 1 and Paper 2, you need to demonstrate your range of knowledge and apply your understanding in short answer and essay responses. You will be tested on what you have learned over your entire course, so it is important to prepare for the types of questions that you will be asked.

SHOWING WHAT YOU KNOW

In this section, some model student answers have been shown to give you an idea of what type of answer you could give in the exam. Before looking at the example answers, try answering the exam-style questions by yourself first. Then compare your answers with the answers given. Check to see if there are places where you could have communicated more effectively or used more appropriate language and terms.

Your Paper 1 questions

There are three sections in Paper 1: Section A, Section B and Section C. You must answer five questions from a total choice of nine. You must choose at least **one** question from Section A, **one** from Section B and **one** from Section C.

Each question has a part (a) and (b) and you must answer both parts. We have given you examples of full-mark answers for a selection of example Paper 1 question below, so you can get familiar with the question types and how to best approach them. Four example questions have been selected at random for this section to give you an idea of how to to answer the questions in Paper 1.

Hinduism

1. 'Those who remember me at the time of death will come to me. Do not doubt this. Whatever occupies the mind at the time of death determines the destination of dying; always they will tend towards that state of being. Therefore remember me at all times and fight on. With your heart and mind one-pointed through regular practice of meditation, you will find the supreme glory of the Lord.'

   Bhagavad Gita

   (a) Identify **three** beliefs which can be found within the above passage. **[3]**

   One belief that can be found in the passage is reverence for the supreme Lord, Brahman, who will reward the practitioner at their time of death if they worship him. This will eventually allow an individual to find 'the supreme glory of the Lord' and reach moksha, or the release from the endless cycle of birth and rebirth, samsara. That the occupation of the mind at the time of death 'determines the destination of dying' is the belief of karma, or the force generated by one's actions. Another belief is in yoga, which is referred to as meditation, since yoga can be done through physical or mental activity.

ANSWER ANALYSIS

- This response addresses the question by using specific content to identify three specific beliefs.
- Each sentence includes a different belief with new vocabulary words that are clearly defined.
- All sentences fully explain how that content relates to the question.
- The responses clarify which part of the text is being referenced to fully answer the question. This student has identified three clear beliefs, for three marks.

In Paper 1, you should use religious vocabulary to develop an individual idea that can stand on its own. Make sure the idea is relevant to the question being asked, not just relevant to the religion.

You will not have studied all the religions included in the exam. Choose the questions you are best prepared to answer based on your studies, regardless of your own personal religious or secular background.

For example, you could answer:
- one question from Section A
- three questions from Section B
- one question from Section C.

Questions on Hinduism will appear in Section A.

Different terms and phrases are used to reference Brahman, the supreme God in Hinduism. Here, 'Lord' is used to reference Brahman, but at other times it may also be read as 'eternal truth'.

Defining the term fully and referencing a portion of the passage in which it is written helps demonstrate your understanding.

IDENTIFY

Pick out specific pieces of information from the passage.

(b) Explain how one might 'find the supreme glory of the Lord' and embark upon the path to moksha through yoga? **[6]**

Participating in yoga is a way that a Hindu practitioner can reach Brahman and find supreme glory in him. There are multiple yogic paths, given that Hinduism is a religion of pluralism, allowing for multiple ways to reach one's religious goals, but there are four main paths that individuals usually choose. One type of yoga is Bhakti yoga, which is a practice done through compassion and love for others. Through conducting acts of kindness, one can find Brahman through a path focused on love. Another path is karma yoga, which is the path of action, which deals with the law of cause and effect, and involves a person embarking on purposeful actions throughout their life with pure intentions. Another path is Raja yoga, which involves actions of self-discipline, either physical or mental, through asanas and pranayama breathing. The last path is through Gyana yoga, which is the philosophical path, which involves acquiring knowledge through study and practice. By participating in yoga, Hindu practitioners can actively seek union with Brahman, and join their inner atman, or soul, with the Supreme God Force through a path of their choice. Ultimately, this ends the cycle of samsara and allows a practitioner to achieve moksha, thereby finding the 'supreme glory of the lord'.

ANSWER ANALYSIS

When you start preparing for the Paper 2 exam, think 'how do we get there?' when you are writing your answers. Remember that the answers to the three essential questions are what examiners are wanting to see demonstration of, particularly knowledge and analysis.

EXPLAIN

Write a detailed response, including answering 'how' or 'why'.

There are many yogic paths a Hindu practitioner can embark upon, but there are four major paths that are usually followed. These will be chosen based on the practitioner's personality or preferences. Since this is a six-mark response, be sure to describe each yogic path succinctly.

While answering a question on yoga or moksha, check that you've included an explanation of 'atman'. This is the soul or essence of divinity within Hindu practitioners that will reach union with Brahman through yoga, after moksha is achieved.

ANSWER ANALYSIS

- Full sentences are used and the answer is logically structured.
- Question is addressed throughout, for example, 'moksha through yoga'.
- Relevant terminology is used throughout the response with at least one specific, clearly defined vocabulary word in each sentence to achieve 6 marks.
- The response thoroughly explains key aspects of Buddhism and focuses on types of yoga.
- The response acknowledges that there are several ways to 'find the supreme glory of the Lord' and discusses the four main paths.

Buddhism

2. 'Disenchanted, he becomes dispassionate. Through dispassion, he is fully released. With full release, there is the knowledge, 'Fully released.' He discerns that 'Birth is ended, the holy life fulfilled, the task done. There is nothing further for this world.'

Adittapariyaya Sutta

(a) Identify **three** beliefs present in the above passage. **[3]**

One belief presented in the passage is the process of enlightenment, which is represented by being fully released and thereby acquiring knowledge. Another belief present is samsara, or the cycle of birth and rebirth. In the portion where it says, 'birth is ended', it means the cycle of samsara has ended. Lastly, nirvana, or the release from the cycle of samsara is represented, in the portion that states 'there is nothing further for this world'.

(b) Explain how a Buddhist practitioner may embark upon a path in which they were 'fully released'. **[6]**

Buddhist practitioners can embark upon a path of being 'fully released' – or, in other words, reaching nirvana – through living one's life according to Buddhist doctrine, such as The Four Noble Truths and the Eightfold Path. The Four Noble Truths, one of Buddhism's most important doctrines, calls upon practitioners to understand that life is suffering (or dukkha), according to the First Noble Truth, and that suffering is caused by desire (or tanha) or unhealthy attachments to things in life that are impermanent. The Third Noble Truth is that there is a way to cease one's suffering which lies in the Fourth Noble Truth – the way to cease suffering is through following the Eightfold Path. Before embarking upon the Eightfold Path, a person must commit, apply sati, or mindfulness and orient themselves toward Right Association. Right Association is a preliminary step before beginning the Eightfold Path, which requires a practitioner to be fully ready mentally and emotionally before beginning the rest of the steps on the path. The rest of the Eightfold Path has a person adopting steps from 'Right Livelihood' to 'Right Action', which calls upon them to adhere to the Eightfold Path in a way where they can move through the world in a balanced fashion, with the components of the path on their mind while living their everyday lives. A practitioner, after moving successfully through the components of the Eightfold Path, which may take lifetimes, then achieves nirvana.

Questions on Buddhism will appear in Section A.

There are multiple ways in which 'enlightenment' might be referenced in Buddhism. Here it is referenced as 'knowledge', but you should be ready to identify it within passages in other various forms, such as 'awakening' or 'awareness'.

There are also multiple ways in which 'nirvana' might be referenced in Buddhism. If nirvana is the official end to the cycle of birth and rebirth that is samsara, then other terms might be used to reference this end, such as 'release' or 'escape'.

It is necessary to recognize the meanings of Buddhist terms in Sanskrit. Here, mindfulness is referenced as *sati*. You should be prepared to recognize major Buddhist terms in both Sanskrit and English, as many times the English version of the term will not be provided.

Judaism

4. 'And at that time there will be no hunger or war, no jealousy or rivalry. For the good will be plentiful, and all delicacies available as dust. The entire occupation of the world will be only to know God... the people Israel will be of great wisdom; they will perceive the esoteric truths and comprehend their Creator's wisdom as is the capacity of man.'

Maimonides, Mishneh Torah

(a) Identify **three** teachings in this passage. [3]

- People are expected to prepare for the Messianic Age which will be a peaceful time of brotherhood on earth.

- Jewish practitioners believe that the Messiah will come to gather the chosen people to redeem them.

- To prepare for the Messianic Age, Jewish practitioners believe in practicing tikkun olam, which is the act of doing good deeds to restore the world with the goal of perfecting it for the world to come.

(b) Explain Jewish teachings about the world to come. [6]

Jewish practitioners believe that God gave humans free will to make their own decisions in this life, and that those decisions can impact the world to come. Practitioners should prepare for this time by doing good works and showing good inclination (yetzer hatov) instead of having bad inclination (yetzer hara).

Practitioners have increased responsibility within the Jewish community to do good deeds after their bar/bat mitzvah (coming of age ceremony) and there is an expectation that they have matured and no longer have yetzer ha-ra. Jewish practitioners are expected to observe Shabbat (a day of rest) in order to reflect on their covenant with God, remember that God brought the Jewish people out of Egypt, and to prepare for the Messianic Age. As a member of the Jewish community, practitioners adhere to God's will because He has commanded them to do so. When Jewish practitioners and adherents perform tikkun olam, restoring the world, they also prepare for the world to come.

Jewish practitioners can strengthen their relationship with God in order to prepare for the world to come by seeking guidance from their synagogue's rabbi (religious leader) and studying the Torah, the central religious text in Judaism. Many practitioners

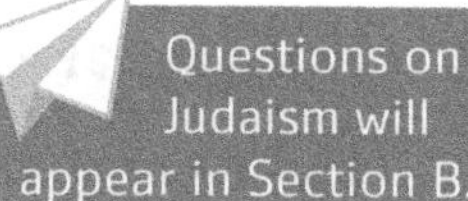

Questions on Judaism will appear in Section B.

ANSWER ANALYSIS

- This question is answered using specific content in three bullet points.
- Each bullet point included new vocabulary and fully identifies a teaching as it connects to the quote.
- Even though it was written in bullet points, the response included clearly developed full sentences that demonstrate content knowledge specific to the question.

EXPLAIN

Provide a detailed description or summary with reasons or causes.

God and significant religious figures are usually capitalized (God instead of god) to acknowledge their sacredness within the religion. Often the pronoun 'He' is used, although this more closely relates to the language in which the religion was established rather than ascribing a gender. As with the usage of 'God,' the pronoun 'He' should be capitalized as well. IB students who take this exam may choose to write G-d to acknowledge the sanctity of monotheism in Judaism. However, you will not lose points for not doing so.

engage in Daf Yomi, the daily study of the Torah in sections, that takes seven years to complete. A Jewish practitioner may also seek to study the Talmud, which provides rabbinical commentary on the Torah, in order to strengthen their relationship with God and prepare for the world to come. It is important to note that the movements of Judaism do not agree about the Messianic Age and that many Reform Jewish practitioners may not subscribe to this aspect of Judaism, whereas many Orthodox Jewish practitioners do believe in the Messianic Age.

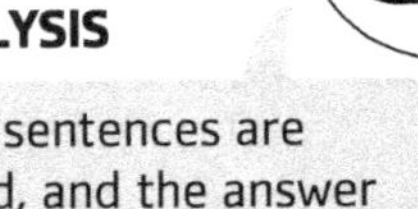

ANSWER ANALYSIS

Full sentences are used, and the answer is logically structured.

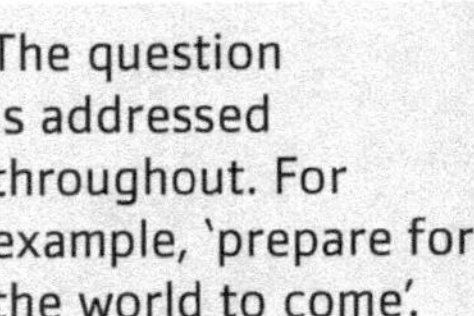

ANSWER ANALYSIS

The question is addressed throughout. For example, 'prepare for the world to come'.

ANSWER ANALYSIS

- The response addresses different ways to answer the question and explains different aspects of Judaism.
- Appropriate answers are used ('Shabbat') and justified with an explanation ('in order to reflect on their covenant with God').
- Answer is well developed (explaining how coming of age changes perception of good deeds).

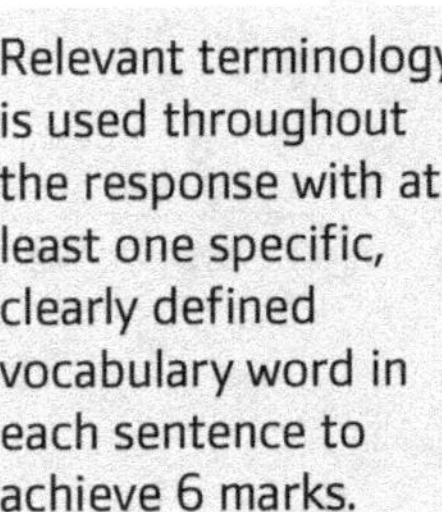

ANSWER ANALYSIS

Relevant terminology is used throughout the response with at least one specific, clearly defined vocabulary word in each sentence to achieve 6 marks.

Islam

6. 'That is Allah, your Lord; there is no deity except Him, the Creator of all things, so worship Him. And He is Disposer of all things.'

Surah 6:102

The concept of oneness, or *tawhid*, is referenced in the text even though it doesn't appear in the text.

(a) Outline **three** teachings in this passage. [3]

- In Islam practitioners must hold Allah as sacred and recognize that he is the 'Creator of all things'.
- Practitioners must accept tawhid, the concept of Allah's oneness, which is central to monotheism in Islam, and is referenced in the phrase 'there is no deity except Him'.
- The oneness of God alludes to Shahada, the first pillar in Islam, which is the confession of faith that there is no God but Allah, and that the prophet Muhammad (PBUH) is his messenger.

Questions on Islam will appear in Section B.

OUTLINE

Briefly describe or summarize.

Some bullet points reference a brief, specific part of the text using 'Creator of all things' and others allude to the specific section of the text, such as discussing 'oneness'.

ANSWER ANALYSIS

- The question is addressed by using detailed content in three bullet points that are specific to both the religion and the text.
- Each bullet point included new vocabulary and fully explained how that content related to the question.
- Even in bullet points, the answer has clearly developed sentences.

(b) Explain the ways in which a Muslim shows devotion to Allah. **[6]**

Practitioners of Islam show their devotion to Allah by submitting to his will, which was revealed to the prophet Muhammad (PBUH) through the Qur'an, the sacred text of Islam. It is important that practitioners and adherents of Islam show their devotion to Allah because the nature of Allah is of tawhid, or oneness, and He created all things. Practitioners can demonstrate their devotion by following the Five Pillars of Islam: profession of faith, prayer, almsgiving, fasting, and pilgrimage. Even though the Five Pillars are not explicitly stated in the Qur'an, they are mentioned in the Hadith, which is the book of the sayings of the prophet Muhammad (PBUH). Following the guidance set forth in the Hadith is a way of showing one's devotion to Allah. Studying and following the sayings in the Hadith, one follows the perfect life of submission to Allah, the life of the prophet Muhammad (PBUH). In addition to the first pillar (Shahada), prayer (salat) plays a central role in the life of a Muslim, as there is a set way to pray – five times a day facing Mecca – to show one's devotion to Allah. Other ways of showing devotion to Allah are through the pillar of almsgiving (zakat) to give charity to the poor and the pillar of fasting (sawm) to abstain from food, drink and impure behaviours during the month of Ramadan. The final pillar is yet another way that practitioners can show their devotion to Allah by doing pilgrimage (hajj), a journey to Mecca, just as the prophet Muhammad (PBUH) did.

EXPLAIN

Provide a detailed description or summary with reasons or causes.

PBUH is an acronym for Peace Be Upon Him. PBUH is used after writing the prophet Muhammad as a sign of respect in Islam. Students may choose to write PBUH for respect. However, you will not lose points for not doing so.

ANSWER ANALYSIS

- Full sentences are used, and the answer is logically structured.
- The question is addressed throughout. For example, the student uses the words 'devotion to Allah' several times.
- Relevant terminology is used with at least one clearly defined vocabulary word in each sentence to achieve 6 marks.

ANSWER ANALYSIS

- The response thoroughly explains key aspects of Islam and defines the Five Pillars, rather than assuming the reader knows this term.
- It addresses different ways to answer the question including through textual study of the Qur'an, yearly observances of the religion (Ramadan), and daily devotion to Allah (prayer).

Your Paper 2 questions

In Paper 2, you will choose two questions to answer out of a possible 14. These are all on guiding themes and you will need to read them carefully before deciding which two to tackle. Let's take a look at some example questions and answers so you can get a better understanding of the type of answer you can give for these Paper 2 questions.

Section A

Judaism

1. To what extent are all Jewish practitioners expected to follow the Torah? [15]

Judaism has persevered and has been preserved as the oldest of the Abrahamic religions because of its strong foundation. This foundation is the word of G-d in the form of the Torah. According to Jewish practitioners, Moses received the Torah on Mount Sinai. The Torah is the Pentateuch of five books: Genesis, Exodus, Leviticus, Numbers, and Deuteronomy. According to Jewish practitioners, the Torah was delivered to Moses on Mount Sinai by G-d after He delivered the Israelites out of slavery in Egypt after the tenth plague. The Torah is a central part of the religion because it provides laws and guidance for practitioners to follow and is used to strengthen their relationship with G-d. As such, the idea that all Jewish practitioners should be expected to follow the Torah seems to be accurate. However, as Judaism has developed for thousands of years, Jewish practitioners have changed and developed as well. While some movements within Judaism and some individual practitioners believe that the Torah must be followed and should be followed literally, other movements and individuals do not. This hints at the diversity of the Jewish community and this topic plays a central role in the disagreements among the major movements within Judaism.

   The Torah includes 613 mitzvot (commandments) that Jewish practitioners should follow. These commandments include everyday life such as kashrut laws, which detail the dietary restrictions and determine the foods that Jewish practitioners can eat, the kosher foods. While Jewish practitioners are expected to follow the teachings of the Torah, some may choose not to. This is because in some movements, especially Reform Judaism, Jewish practitioners are still considered to be Jewish regardless of their actions because they are G-d's chosen people. Jewish practitioners believe in the strength of the religion due to the preservation of the culture and ideals. Rabbi Schneerson once stated that all Jewish practitioners

TO WHAT EXTENT

You need to draw conclusions about the merits or faults of an argument or concept and support this with evidence and sound argument.

ANSWER ANALYSIS

Full sentences are used, and the answer is logically structured. This is a five-paragraph essay with an introductory paragraph that includes a thesis (argument that addresses the question), three-body paragraphs, and a conclusion that goes beyond a restatement of the thesis.

ANSWER ANALYSIS

The question is addressed throughout, for example, 'the extent to which practitioners should adhere to Jewish law'.

ANSWER ANALYSIS

Relevant terminology is used throughout the essay with key concepts explained as well.

have an eternal bond with G-d and that a Jewish practitioner is still Jewish, even if he has committed a sin against G-d. Many within the Reform Judaism movement and many individual practitioners may seek to follow some aspects of the Torah and not others in order to adapt to modern society. An example of this would be whether or not a Jewish practitioner may drive on Shabbat. While many practitioners have chosen to adapt to modern society and maintain a strong connection to G-d and to Judaism, others, especially Orthodox Jewish practitioners, have chosen to maintain a strict adherence to the laws and commandments of the Torah.

For many in the Orthodox Jewish movement, the eternal bond with G-d is not enough, and it is important to follow the laws that are listed in the Torah, including the kashrut laws and observing Shabbat, a day of rest and a time to reflect on G-d. The practitioners should show their gratitude to G-d by practicing their religion and living in accordance with the Torah, the Talmud (the oral Torah), and the Ten Commandments, all of which were received by Moses from G-d on Mount Sinai. Practitioners should show their gratitude to G-d for being His chosen people and for being delivered out of Egypt. This strict adherence to Jewish scriptures represents the determination of Jewish practitioners to preserve the religion and prepare for the world to come. For some in the Orthodox tradition this strict adherence is a deliberate decision to outwardly demonstrate their faith in spite of the persecution that Jewish individuals have faced historically.

Furthermore, Jewish practitioners should also follow the Torah to strengthen their relationship with G-d and to remind them of G-d's covenant with Abraham as detailed in Genesis in the Torah. The Abrahamic Covenant promised land, protection, and many descendants in exchange for following G-d's word. G-d asked Abraham to sacrifice his son Isaac and Abraham was willing to do that because of his faith in G-d. Following the Torah gives Jewish practitioners the opportunity to demonstrate their commitment to G-d. By following the commandments of G-d in the Torah, Jewish practitioners form a deeper connection with G-d and show that despite being given free will, they choose to act in accordance with G-d's will. Finally, Jewish practitioners must use the Torah to implement G-d's plan for the world to come. With the goal of reaching the Messianic Age, a time

ANSWER ANALYSIS

The question acknowledges different interpretations of the question and different answers to the question due to the differences in Jewish movements. This discussion of different interpretations or perspectives ensures higher marks.

ANSWER ANALYSIS

The Torah is referenced generally and specifically, as the essay was able to point to specific sections in the book of Genesis to discuss the 'Abrahamic Covenant'.

ANSWER ANALYSIS

A text by a rabbi was referenced for additional perspective.

If you don't know a term used in this response or question, look it up in your notes before your exam to help you with your revision.

of peace and brotherhood on earth, practitioners should adhere to the Torah and follow tikkun olam and do good deeds with the goal of repairing the world. Jewish practitioners receive guidance and laws on how to reach the Messianic Age by following the Torah.

While some practitioners of Judaism believe that all Jews must strictly practice the teachings of the Torah, other practitioners may disagree due to social circumstances and divisions among the major movements of Judaism. Debates continue about the extent to which practitioners should follow the Torah; however, a key feature of a Jewish practitioner is simply that they have an eternal bond with G-d, whether they strictly adhere to the Torah or not.

This is a great example of a concluding sentence that goes beyond restating the thesis!

Buddhism

2. Using Buddhist doctrine and beliefs, examine the role that sati plays in the lives of Buddhist practitioners. [15]

Within Buddhism, tanha, or desiring and craving, is one of the sufferings humans endure according to Buddhism's founder Siddhartha Gautama and The Four Noble Truths. However, in order to conquer and eliminate these sufferings, the Buddha instructed that people must employ sati, or mindfulness, when living their lives and attempting to overcome suffering. The concept of sati can be seen as a core foundation of Buddhism in different Buddhist doctrines and beliefs, such as within The Four Noble Truths, the Eightfold Path, and throughout the meditation process the Buddha underwent in order to attain enlightenment and nirvana.

The Four Noble Truths embody the belief in sati as they remind practitioners about the sufferings of themselves and the world: while offering a way to overcome life's sufferings. The First Noble Truth states very simply that life is suffering, or dukkha. This, according to the Buddha, is a reality that we must all accept and face. The Second Noble Truth states that there is a cause of life's suffering, which usually revolves around desire, or tanha. Many of life's sufferings arise because of the impermanence of unhealthy desires or attachment to parts of life that are impermanent. All of life exists in an impermanent state and is subject to change. This allows for practitioners to be alert about their surroundings as everything from objects to relationships to their existence on this earth is subject to change. Therefore, if a person has an unhealthy attachment to that which is impermanent,

Be prepared to relate vocabulary terms (Sanskrit or English) to multiple pieces of doctrine. Here, you are being asked to relate sati, or mindfulness, to different forms of doctrine. This means you must be able to fully describe examples of doctrine such as the Four Noble Truths and Eightfold Path so that you can analyse their connections to various Buddhist principles.

Since this prompt is open-ended, you should briefly brainstorm the numerous examples of Buddhist doctrine and principles that you could possibly write about. After you've generated a short list, consider the ways in which sati can best relate to all of them.

they will be plagued with tanha, in which they will desire things like a return to the past, a replenishment of material wealth, or the continual existence of a significant relationship. The Third Noble Truth is that there is a way to cease or end one's suffering. However, this involves sati and awareness because the individual must realize in extreme conditions that there is a way for their suffering to stop. Such extreme conditions might include drug or alcohol abuse, intense mourning, or suicidal thoughts. Individuals must demonstrate that they are in a negative condition and have a healthy desire to make the right decision. The way to end suffering is through the Fourth Noble Truth, which is the Eightfold Path. The Eightfold Path, or The Middle Way, is a path that allows practitioners to relieve their pain and suffering, eventually attaining nirvana, or an escape from samsara, the continual birth and rebirth of life. The Eightfold Path consists of both ascetic and non-ascetic ideals. Some of the conditions that the Eightfold Path encourages on the path are 'right mindfulness' and 'right actions', which demonstrates a need for a practitioner to be mindful. This is because it is only through mental discipline and focus that a practitioner will be able to change their mental condition in order to create change for themselves. Therefore, the Four Noble Truths embodies sati as it reminds practitioners to be aware that their environment is full of suffering and change and that nirvana can be attained through the Eightfold Path.

On the other hand, the Eightfold Path also emphasizes sati as it provides guidelines for practitioners to have right actions and right thoughts. One aspect of the Eightfold Path states 'Right Conduct' which is that one should perform good deeds and not harm anything or anyone. From this, an example is the Five Precepts to which a practitioner must adhere and apply to their daily lives. The Five Precepts state: no killing, no sexual misconduct, no stealing, no harmful language, and no consuming intoxicants. Thus, this encourages individuals who abide by the Five Precepts to be mindful in their everyday lives to not do harmful deeds to others and themselves, either consciously or subconsciously. By prohibiting these actions, practitioners can avoid tanha and be more conscious and mindful of their lives, actions, and goals within Buddhism. Also, the Eightfold path explicitly states 'Right Mindfulness' which means that people should not only be mindful, but

ANSWER ANALYSIS

The Sanskrit term sati is defined and connected to Buddhist doctrine and principle throughout the entirety of the paper.

ANSWER ANALYSIS

A command of other Buddhist vocabulary terms is shown when relevant and in connection to sati. Terminology is defined and connections are explained.

ANSWER ANALYSIS

Buddhist doctrine (the Four Noble Truths, Eightfold Path, and Precepts) are all fully and specifically explained.

ANSWER ANALYSIS

An understanding of the life of Siddhartha Guatama is shown, and used in connection with meditation practices which require sati.

mindful with the correct thoughts. Similarly, 'Right Concentration' tells practitioners that whenever they are faced with a task, they must wholeheartedly devote their attention towards it, which is what 'sati' encompasses. Therefore, sati is shown within the Eightfold Path as it reminds practitioners about conducting moral actions, thoughts, and focus.

Lastly, sati can be seen within meditation practices, most obviously within the Buddha's meditation pathway to Enlightenment. When the Buddha was meditating, he remained conscious of all his thoughts and noted any patterns he observed. For example, whenever the Buddha was caught in a distracting thought cycle instead of dismissing it, he would count how many times a distracting thought appeared. This demonstrates sati as the Buddha was mindful of how many times his thoughts became distracting. Additionally, within Buddhism, there is a form of meditation where a practitioner focuses on their breathing, which some refer to as Pranayama Breathing (existing in both Hinduism and Buddhism). The meditator will slowly breathe, while counting in increments of ten, and exhibiting an awareness of how many breaths they took. Another form of meditation is having a focal point or object, in which the meditator can imagine an object within their minds or directly in front of them and focus their attention upon it. These two forms of meditation also embody sati as it requires a great amount of concentration and consciousness to perform these forms of meditations properly. Thus, meditation also reflects sati as mindfulness is required in order to produce the best results and have a successful meditation session.

In conclusion, sati plays an essential role in Buddhist beliefs and doctrine, and therefore in the everyday lives of Buddhist practitioners. Through the Four Noble Truths, the Eightfold Path, and meditation practice, a practitioner can exhibit mindfulness, relieve their sufferings, and eventually attain enlightenment and nirvana, as modelled by Siddhartha Gautama, the original Buddha.

TESTING WHAT YOU KNOW

Set A

In this section, you will be able to test yourself with different sets of practice papers under exam conditions. By taking these mock papers, you will build your confidence and be able to identify any areas you need a bit more practice on. Set A Paper 1 and Paper 2 have a lot of additional guidance in the margin to help you get to the right answer, so attempt Set A first.

All you need is this book, a timer, a pen and some extra paper to use if you run out of answer lines. Then you can check your answers at the back of the book when you're done. Take a deep breath, set your timer, and good luck!

Paper 1

Set your timer for 1 hour 15 minutes.

Answer a total of **five** questions, selecting **at least one** from **each** section (A, B and C).

Section A

Answer **at least one** question.

Hinduism

Study the passage below and answer the questions which follow.

1.

> This is my lower nature;
> But beyond this, I have another,
> Higher nature; the life
> That sustains all beings in the world
>
> Know that it is the womb
> From which all beings arise;
> The universe is born within me,
> And within me will be destroyed.

The Bhagavad Gita

(a) Identify **three** beliefs present in this passage. **[3]**

Your answers will be scored based on a 'best fit' model for the responses. Examiners are looking for accurate and relevant responses. They use question-specific mark schemes to score the Paper 1 responses and markbands, or 'grade boundaries' to determine the most accurate score for Paper 2.

IDENTIFY

Write an answer from multiple possibilities.

In Paper 1, you will be asked to **identify** or **outline** in part (a), then **explain** and make connections in part (b).

You can use bullet points in part (a) to make sure that you are writing clear, simple responses.

Pull out the key words from the passage that will help you in creating a detailed, specific answer.

Make sure you describe beliefs from **this passage**. You will not get marks for your own knowledge in part (a).

AO1: Part (a) of this question asks you to show knowledge and understanding of specific content from a religion by responding to a question that follows a short text related to that religion.

(b) Explain what is meant by 'This is my lower nature;/But beyond this, I have another,/Higher nature; the life/That sustains all beings in the world'.　　**[6]**

You could explain the limitless power of Brahman, connecting God to the continual destruction and rebirth of the world.

Expanding upon the conception that Brahman is infinite and formless, you could further discuss the inter-cooperation between deities within the Trimurti, and their existence as being extensions of Brahman's limitless powers.

Remember to keep referring to the quote given in the question as you need to keep your answer on topic.

Do not repeat the same points from part (a) in part (b). However, you can build off those points and elaborate.

EXPLAIN

In Paper 1, the part (b) question will always use 'Explain' as the command term. You will need to give a detailed description or summary with reasons or causes.

AO2: Part (b) of this question asks you to show your understanding by applying your content knowledge as it relates to the text and to analyse how that information connects to the essential questions for that religion.

Buddhism

Study the passage below and answer the questions which follow.

2. 'Alas, all living things wear themselves out. Over and over again they are born, they age and die, and pass on to a new life, and are reborn. What is more, greed and false hopes blind them and they are blind from birth. Frightened, they do not yet know how to get out of this great ill.'

Siddhartha Guatama

(a) Outline **three** beliefs found within this passage. **[3]**

(b) Explain the connection between the concept of tanha and samsara. **[6]**

Do not rewrite the quote in your answer. It will waste your time and you will not get any marks for it. Just pull out the key words.

Define samsara and explain the idea of attachment in Buddhism, along with craving or desire, or tanha.

Don't spend too much time on your 3-mark answers, keep them short but specific.

Use the word 'practitioners' to refer to the people of a specific religious group (such as Buddhist practitioners).

Expand on the connection between samsara and tanha by including the types of cravings, desires, or attachments that individuals are plagued by and connect them to the concept of suffering, or dukkha, in Buddhism.

Expand on the continuation of samsara and the eventual goal of achieving nirvana and enlightenment.

Sikhism

Study the passage below and answer the questions which follow.

3.   'Oh Mohan, at the very last moment of life, death shall not approach You.

All who worship You in thought, word and deed shall obtain Your Gifts.
Even the impure, the stupid and the foolish obtain Divine Knowledge upon
seeing You. Says Nanak, Oh God, You are present within all,
You are above all.'

Guru Granth Sahib

(a) Identify **three** Sikh teachings represented in this passage.   **[3]**

(b) Explain how a Sikh practitioner envisions the nature of God.   **[6]**

Write an answer from multiple possibilities.

You should describe concepts such as maya and haumai.
You could also briefly describe the concept of jot.

Remember to pull out the key words of the quote to avoid rewriting it in your answer.

Describe the difference between gurmukh and manmukh. Gurmukh is a necessary condition in order to understand God and live in accordance with the teachings of the gurus.

Think about man's emotions, or the lower emotions. How do they compare to higher-level emotions which allow us to achieve union with God? How do they differ with the nature of God? How can you add this into your answer?

Ensure you accurately use relevant terminology throughout your answer.

Don't forget which religion you are writing about in your answer. You don't want to mix key beliefs up!

Section B

Answer **at least one** question.

Judaism

Study the passage below and answer the questions which follow.

4. 'Anyone who injures their neighbor is to be injured in the same manner: fracture for fracture, eye for eye, tooth for tooth. The one who has inflicted the injury must suffer the same injury.'

Leviticus 24:19–21

(a) Outline **three** teachings from this passage. **[3]**

(b) Explain the role of Jewish law in the lives of Jewish practitioners. **[6]**

OUTLINE

Briefly describe or summarize.

Focus on key words and phrases: 'neighbor', 'injury', and 'suffer the same'.

Do not bring your personal beliefs into your answer, keep your writing impartial.

EXPLAIN

Provide a detailed description or summary with reasons or causes.

Think about appropriate punishments.

Think about the significance of this passage and the book of Leviticus in describing the laws by which Jewish practitioners must live.

Consider the ways that Jewish individuals practise their religion. The specific rituals as well as daily life are often guided by religious laws in Judaism.

Think about the differences in the major movements of Judaism: Orthodox, Conservative, and Reform.

This passage focuses on consequences for actions. You could consider both intentional and unintentional wrongdoings.

Christianity

Study the passage below and answer the questions which follow.

5. 'If I speak in the tongues of men or of angels, but do not have love, I am only a resounding gong or a clanging cymbal. If I have the gift of prophecy and can fathom all mysteries and all knowledge, and if I have a faith that can move mountains, but do not have love, I am nothing. If I give all I possess to the poor and give over my body to hardship that I may boast,[b] but do not have love, I gain nothing.'

1 Corinthians 13:1–3

(a) Identify **three** teachings from this passage. **[3]**

(b) Explain what this passage tells us about the relationship between God and Christian practitioners both on earth and in the afterlife. **[6]**

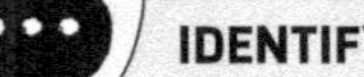

IDENTIFY

Write an answer from multiple possibilities.

With a longer text, you may want to underline the sections that you can connect to specific content and reference those phrases in your response.

The focus is to clearly and simply explain the teaching in your own words. Each teaching connects to the importance of love, showing the central nature of love in Christianity.

Underline the teachings in the passage so you can easily refer to the key words when you are writing.

EXPLAIN

Provide a detailed description or summary with reasons or causes.

Consider Christian beliefs about the afterlife and how Christian practitioners can go to heaven.

Consider Christian beliefs about a Christian's relationship with God through going to Mass and prayer.

Choose some phrases from the passage that represent the question well so you can analyse it thoroughly.

Consider the differences in Christian denominations, especially between Catholicism and Protestantism, to brainstorm a wide range of relevant examples.

Islam

Study the passage below and answer the questions which follow.

6. 'Our Lord, indeed You know what we conceal and what we declare, and nothing is hidden from Allah on the earth or in the heaven.'

Surah 14:38

(a) Outline **three** teachings from this text. [3]

(b) Explain how the above passage relates to the overall goals of Islam, and how a practitioner might achieve those goals. [6]

Section C

Answer **at least one** question.

Taoism

Study the passage below and answer the questions which follow.

7. 'Those who try to control, who use force to protect their power, go against the direction of the Tao. They take from those who don't have enough and give to those who have far too much.

    The Master can keep giving because there is no end to her wealth. She acts without expectation, succeeds without taking credit, and doesn't think that she is better than anyone else.'

    Lao Tzu

    (a) Outline **three** Taoist beliefs that are represented in this passage.   **[3]**

    (b) Explain how the above passage relates to the overall goals of Taoism, and how a practitioner might go about achieving those goals.   **[6]**

OUTLINE

Briefly describe or summarize.

AO1: Part (a) of this question asks you to show knowledge and understanding of specific content from a religion by responding to a question that follows a short text related to that religion.

You could consider the concept of wu wei.

Consider how Taoist teachings might symbolically relate to three different components of the passage.

In Paper 1 questions, consider the source of the text and how that may impact your response.

EXPLAIN

Provide a detailed description or summary with reasons or causes.

In this passage, consider how a Taoist practitioner seeks to achieve harmony with the Tao, or the underlying set of principles and force of the universe.

Consider mentioning chi, and mechanisms, like tai chi, used to create balance and harmony in the universe.

Describe concepts like yin and yang and fu, and how they relate to balance, order, and returning to the source.

Jainism

Study the passage below and answer the questions which follow.

8. 'Do unto others as you would like to be done by. Injury or violence done by you to any life in any form, animal or human, is as harmful as it would be if caused to your own self.'

Lord Mahavira

(a) Outline **three** teachings in this passage. [3]

(b) Explain how the passage relates to the goals of Jainism, and how a practitioner might go about achieving those goals. [6]

Bahá'i Faith

Study the passage below and answer the questions which follow.

9. 'The utterance of God is a lamp, whose light is these words: Ye are the fruits of one tree, and the leaves of one branch. Deal ye one with another with the utmost love and harmony, with friendliness and fellowship. ... So powerful is the light of unity that it can illuminate the whole earth.'

Bahá'u'lláh, Epistle to the Son of the Wolf

(a) Identify **three** teachings in this passage.　　　　　　　　　　[3]

(b) Explain Bahá'i beliefs on unity.　　　　　　　　　　[6]

> **IDENTIFY**
> Write an answer from multiple possibilities.

You could discuss the oneness of God, humanity, and religion as it is central to the Bahá'i faith.

Before you begin your answer, make sure you have chosen which three teachings you are going to write about.

Don't feel pressure to start writing immediately. Always think about what you want to say first so you can execute your answer in the best way possible.

> **EXPLAIN**
> Provide a detailed description or summary with reasons or causes.

Expand on ideas of oneness and make connections to the unity that the Bahá'i faith has with other religions.

Focus on the key word 'unity' – what connotations does it have?

After identifying the beliefs on unity, consider what rituals and practices are a result of these beliefs on unity.

Since unity is central to the Bahá'i faith, you may want to jot down what you know about the religion before you get started on your answer. This can help you determine the specific terminology and content to use in your response.

That's it – your first Paper 1 practice is complete! Don't worry if you went over your timer. Reading the additional tips takes extra time. Make a note of any areas you found difficult and focus on those for your revision in the next few days. Make sure you take a bit of a break – don't go straight into Paper 2. It's important to recharge!

Set A
Paper 2

Set your timer for 1 hour 30 minutes.
You will choose one question from Section A and one question from Section B.
Each question is worth 15 marks.

Section A

Answer **one** question from this section.

Hinduism

1. To what extent is murti the most appropriate mechanism to aid a practitioner in achieving darshan in Hinduism? **[15]**

TO WHAT EXTENT

Write a detailed response with multiple arguments and consider the strengths and weaknesses of each argument.

AO1–AO4

Paper 2 questions test Assessment Objectives 1–3 by asking candidates to write in-depth essay responses that show knowledge (AO1), analysis (AO2), evaluation and synthesis (AO3), and appropriate skills (AO4). Paper 2 assesses all 4 AOs.

In Paper 2, you should use religious vocabulary extensively and connect paragraphs to the three essential questions when appropriate.

You will want to discuss the concept of darshan as it relates to a practitioner's connection or union with Brahman.

When discussing specific content, it is not necessary (or appropriate) to memorize and include direct quotes. Instead, reference the text or author of detailed information when you can.

You could examine the role of murti in aiding this process, but also other mechanisms which might allow a practitioner to experience darshan: being outdoors, or connecting with a temple, priest or guru.

In what ways is murti not the most appropriate mechanism?

Remember to consider both sides of an argument.

ANSWER ANALYSIS

Remember to examine the question from different denominational standpoints. This will better help you to present different sides to the question and get higher marks. Denominational differences may include those which are primarily doctrinal, or ones that are more geographic and cultural by difference.

Continue on to another piece of paper if you need to...

2. Discuss whether moksha could be considered the primary goal in the life of a Hindu practitioner. **[15]**

DISCUSS

Write a detailed response that considers a range of perspectives, arguments, and factors with conclusions supported with evidence.

Define moksha and describe its significant relationship to the cycle of samsara in the life of a Hindu practitioner.

You should also discuss the other goals that a Hindu practitioner must work toward simultaneously while considering the end goal of moksha: dharmic and karmic duty.

Review the key themes from the religions you studied in-depth.

The format of your responses should be a five-paragraph essay structure:
- introductory paragraph with an argument
- at least three body paragraphs about the content
- and a conclusion that restates how you answered the question.

For top marks, you need to demonstrate you have detailed knowledge and understanding of the religion's teachings, beliefs, concepts and practices from multiple standpoints.

Remember to structure your answer clearly and don't jump from one point to another. Keep it linear and precise.

Consider what is meant by the 'primary goal'. Is it important? What are the advantages and disadvantages of and how would it affect a practitioner's life?

Continue on to another piece of paper if you need to...

Buddhism

3. Analyse the significance of the sangha in Buddhism.   [15]

Continue on to another piece of paper if you need to...

4. To what extent are the Theravada and Mahayana similar schools of Buddhist thought in regard to belief and practice? **[15]**

TO WHAT EXTENT

Write a detailed response with multiple arguments and consider the strengths and weaknesses of each argument.

For about five minutes at the start of your exam, start planning by jotting down any information that you may want to include:
- religious vocabulary
- key content
- themes.

To fully answer this question, you will need to discuss both similarities and differences between the two schools of thought.

Ensure that the similar and contrasting information you discuss supports the wording of your argument.

You might want to explain what you think are the most significant pieces of doctrine that both schools of thought adhere to, such as the Four Noble Truths and the Eightfold Path.

Continue on to another piece of paper if you need to…

Sikhism

5. To what extent are the foundational beliefs of Guru Nanak the most significant to the lives of Sikh practitioners? **[15]**

Continue on to another piece of paper if you need to...

6. Discuss the role scripture plays in the social and political life of a Sikh practitioner. **[15]**

Continue on to another piece of paper if you need to...

Open-ended question

7. With reference to **one** religion, **either** Buddhism **or** Hinduism **or** Sikhism, discuss the ways in which beliefs of the afterlife affect the lives of a practitioner. **[15]**

DISCUSS

Write a detailed response that considers a range of perspectives, arguments, and factors with conclusions supported with evidence.

Think about how beliefs of the afterlife affect a religious practitioner's daily life.

Choose the religion which you feel you can write most descriptively and specifically about.

With the open-ended question, be sure to only choose **one** religion.

You will want to describe ritual practice, and the way in which sacred texts or scripture affect a practitioner's everyday behaviour.

ANSWER ANALYSIS

Your evaluation should be well developed, using points to build your argument.

Continue on to another piece of paper if you need to...

Section B

Answer **one** question from this section.

Judaism

8. Examine the importance of Kosher laws in Judaism. [15]

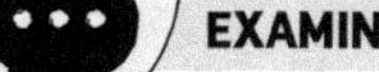

Determine the nature of a concept or claim in detail.

All your Paper 2 questions test how well you show writing techniques with appropriate style to answer the question (AO4).

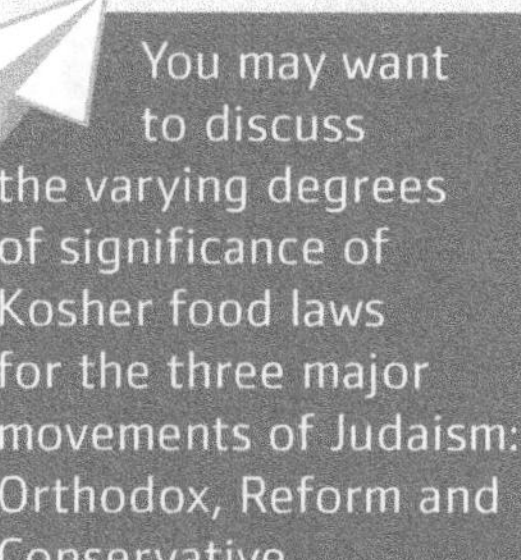

You may want to discuss the varying degrees of significance of Kosher food laws for the three major movements of Judaism: Orthodox, Reform and Conservative.

To show the importance of Kosher food laws, you could compare these to other laws in Judaism.

ANSWER ANALYSIS

Ensure you use relevant terminology throughout your answer.

It's important to mention that the authority of the laws comes directly from the Torah.

Continue on to another piece of paper if you need to…

9. Discuss the significance of the Bar/Bat Mitzvah for the Jewish community. **[15]**

DISCUSS

Write a detailed response that considers a range of perspectives, arguments, and factors with conclusions supported with evidence.

Define what the Bar and Bat Mitzvah are and what they represent.

Discuss the aspects of the Bar/Bat Mitzvah for the individual, such as the preparation and the experience during this ritual and the ways that members of the community support the individual.

Consider the shift in responsibilities for the individual upon being Bar/Bat Mitzvah, and the impact of that shift on the community. Consider both the short-term and long-term impact.

You could write about how various communities, in different parts of the world, may relate to this coming of age ritual. Remember that it is important to define and contextualize community here.

You may want to discuss the Bat Mitzvah being a more recent ritual, and any differences between the Bar and Bat Mitzvah.

Continue on to another piece of paper if you need to...

Christianity

10. Discuss the significance of the sacraments across various denominations of Christianity. [15]

Continue on to another piece of paper if you need to...

11. Examine the role of agape (love) in the lives of Christians. **[15]**

EXAMINE

Determine the nature of a concept or claim in detail.

You may want to break down agape into categories: love of God, the love that Christian practitioners show to God, and the love that Christian practitioners show to other people.

Agape is considered one of the most important aspects of Christian belief.

ANSWER ANALYSIS

Your answer should show a well-structured and reasoned argument, with links between points properly developed.

Think about how many types of love are part of Christian beliefs.

Consider addressing the teaching of Jesus that relates to love. You do not need to memorize specific verses from the Christian bible but it would be useful to review the stories of Jesus from the New Testament.

Islam

12. Discuss the significance of prayer for the umma (entire Muslim community connected by their religion). **[15]**

DISCUSS

Write a detailed response that considers a range of perspectives, arguments, and factors with conclusions supported with evidence.

You may want to start by writing about the significance of prayer within Islam as one of the Five Pillars and the frequency with which practitioners of Islam pray each day.

It is important that you can differentiate between the entire Muslim world, or community, and the specific communities around the world where Islam manifests. Prayer, for example, may have different significance depending on which geographic and cultural community is being discussed. It is important that you can explore this, especially with the command term 'discuss'.

Consider addressing the ways in which Muslim practitioners come together including going to the mosque to pray and facing toward Mecca.

You may also want to establish the significance of the umma within Islam.

ANSWER ANALYSIS

Your conclusion should be supported by the evidence and examples you have used.

13. 'The Qur'an is the only source of authority in Islam.' Discuss. [15]

DISCUSS

Write a detailed response that considers a range of perspectives, arguments and factors with conclusions supported with evidence.

Start with establishing how the Qur'an gets its authority in Islam. Think through the revelation of the Qur'an to the prophet Muhammad (PBUH) through the angel Gabriel.

Discuss the other major religious text for Islam, the Hadith, which provides details on the life of the prophet Muhammad (PBUH) and serves as a source of rules and guidance for Muslims.

You do not need to quote any verses of either the Qur'an or the Hadith, but you should have a clear understanding of the content.

Continue on to another piece of paper if you need to...

Open-ended question

14. With reference to **one** religion, **either** Judaism **or** Christianity **or** Islam, discuss the nature of God. **[15]**

Continue on to another piece of paper if you need to…

Set B

Are you ready to tackle Set B? There are fewer helpful tips and suggestions for this set so make sure you have done some revision in the couple of weeks before you try out these two papers.

Paper 1

Set your timer for 1 hour 15 minutes.

Answer a total of **five** questions, selecting **at least one** from **each** section (A, B and C).

Section A

Make sure at least one of your five questions is from Section A.

Hinduism

Study the passage below and answer the questions which follow.

1. 'According as [the self] acts and according as it behaves, so it becomes: by doing good it becomes good, and by doing evil it becomes evil. It becomes virtuous through virtuous action, and evil through evil action … As is its desire, so is its resolution; and as is its resolution, so is its deed; and whatever deed it does, that it reaps.'

The Vedas

(a) Identify **three** beliefs present in this passage.   [3]

(b) Explain how the passage represents the relationship between karma, samsara and moksha.   [6]

Make sure you take at least a few days' break between Paper 1 and Paper 2. Don't burn yourself out! Have you remembered extra paper in case you run out of writing space?

Remember to pull out the key words from the passage which will help you write an accurate answer.

Read the passage a couple of times before attempting to write your answer.

AO1: Part (a) of this question asks you to show knowledge and understanding of specific content from a religion by responding to a question that follows a short text related to that religion.

IDENTIFY
Write an answer from multiple possibilities.

Think about what each of the key words: 'karma', 'samsara' and 'moksha' mean before writing your answer. Be careful not to mix them up.

Remember to make links amongst the key words in the question throughout your answer so you can achieve full marks.

EXPLAIN
Provide a detailed description or summary with reasons or causes.

Buddhism

Study the passage below and answer the questions which follow.

2. 'The Buddha has explained the cause of all things that arise from a cause.

He, the great monk, has also explained their cessation.'

Buddhist Creed by Senior Monk Prajnaprabha

(a) Identify **three** Buddhist beliefs present in the passage above. **[3]**

(b) Explain the relationship between Buddhist doctrine and 'the cause of all things that arise from a cause' and their 'cessation'. **[6]**

IDENTIFY

Write an answer from multiple possibilities.

AO1: Part (a) of this question asks you to show knowledge and understanding of specific content from a religion by responding to a question that follows a short text related to that religion.

Think about what 'cessation' means in the passage.

Use your own knowledge and examples from the passage to answer the question.

Make sure you write down six different or interconnecting points to gain the marks for this question. You need to make connections to gain high marks.

Don't go off topic. Stick to analysing the quotes and phrases in the question and use your knowledge as supporting evidence.

AO2: Part (b) of this question asks you to show your understanding by applying your content knowledge as it relates to the text and to analyse how that information connects to the essential questions for that religion.

Sikhism

Study the passage below and answer the questions which follow.

3. 'The Guru inculcated love and devotion, the repetition of God's name, and
    the lesson that as men sow so shall they reap. Thus were men saved in every
    direction, and Guru Nanak became the true support of the nine regions of
    the earth.'

Upanishads

(a) Outline **three** Sikh teachings represented in this passage. [3]

(b) Explain how a Sikh practitioner envisions the nature of God. [6]

Section B

Make sure at least one of your five questions is from Section B.

Judaism

Study the passage below and answer the questions which follow.

4. 'And God spoke all these words, saying, "I am the Lord your God, who brought you out of the land of Egypt, out of the house of bondage. You shall have no other gods besides Me."'

Exodus 20:1–3

(a) Outline **three** teachings from this passage. **[3]**

(b) Explain what this passage tells us about the relationship between God and Jewish practitioners. **[6]**

OUTLINE
Briefly describe or summarize.

Make sure that you have listed three separate points and to not spend more than a few minutes on each part (a) question.

Reference the Decalogue, or the Ten Commandments. 'I am the Lord your God' is the first commandment and 'You shall have no other gods before me' is the second commandment.

Don't be tempted to write about the other Ten Commandments that you know. Make sure you focus on what is specifically listed in the question.

EXPLAIN
Provide a detailed description or summary with reasons or causes.

Consider a Jewish practitioner's relationship to the Torah – how do they adhere to it?

Consider what Jewish people consider as the characteristics of God? How is He defined?

AO2: Part (b) of this question asks you to show your understanding by applying your content knowledge as it relates to the text and to analyse how that information connects to the essential questions for that religion.

Christianity

Study the passage below and answer the questions which follow.

5. 'The Lord is my shepherd; I shall not want.

   He maketh me to lie down in green pastures: he leadeth me beside the still waters.

   He restoreth my soul: he leadeth me in the paths of righteousness for his name's sake.

   Yea, though I walk through the valley of the shadow of death, I will fear no evil: for thou art with me; thy rod and thy staff they comfort me.

   Thou preparest a table before me in the presence of mine enemies: thou anointest my head with oil; my cup runneth over.

   Surely goodness and mercy shall follow me all the days of my life: and I will dwell in the house of the LORD for ever.'

   Psalm 23: 1–5

(a) Identify **three** teachings from this passage. **[3]**

(b) Explain how Christian practitioners may 'dwell in the house of the Lord forever'. **[6]**

What does this passage tell you that God provides to Christian practitioners?

Discuss the phrases 'paths of righteousness' and 'goodness and mercy'. What do these reveal about the goals of Christianity?

Do not rewrite the whole passage to demonstrate a point – pull out key phrases.

IDENTIFY

Write an answer from multiple possibilities.

AO1: Part (a) of this question asks you to show knowledge and understanding of specific content from a religion by responding to a question that follows a short text related to that religion.

EXPLAIN

Provide a detailed description or summary with reasons or causes.

Consider the sacraments and their involvement in the Christian faith.

What elements of the Christian faith might help practitioners in leading a fulfilled life?

AO2: Part (b) of this question asks you to show your understanding by applying your content knowledge as it relates to the text and to analyse how that information connects to the essential questions for that religion.

Islam

Study the passage below and answer the questions which follow.

6. He created the heavens and earth in truth. He wraps the night over the day and wraps the day over the night and has subjected the sun and the moon, each running [its course] for a specified term. Unquestionably, He is the Exalted in Might, the Perpetual Forgiver.

Surah 39:5

(a) Identify **three** teachings in this passage. [3]

(b) Explain the beliefs regarding submission in Islam. [6]

IDENTIFY

Write an answer from multiple possibilities.

Consider the concept of tawhid.

Consider the nature of Allah as the creator of everything.

AO1: Part (a) of this question asks you to show knowledge and understanding of specific content from a religion by responding to a question that follows a short text related to that religion.

EXPLAIN

Provide a detailed description or summary with reasons or causes.

Consider the different connotations of the word 'submission'.

Think about the Five Pillars of Islam and how you can relate them to the question.

Don't just write about submission in Islam. Make sure to connect your points to specific sections from the passage.

AO2: Part (b) of this question asks you to show your understanding by applying your content knowledge as it relates to the text and to analyse how that information connects to the essential questions for that religion.

Section C

Make sure at least one of your five questions is from Section C.

Taoism

Study the passage below and answer the questions which follow.

7. 'But when the essence is manifested,
It [The Tao] has a different name.
This same origin is called 'The Profound Mystery.'
As profound as the mystery as It can be,
It is the Gate to the essence of all life.'

Tao Te Ching, Chapter 1

(a) Identify **three** beliefs found in the above passage. **[3]**

(b) Explain how a Taoist practitioner might connect with 'The Profound Mystery' in their lifetime. **[6]**

IDENTIFY

Write an answer from multiple possibilities.

Think about the meaning of 'profound' – could it be a clue?

Don't spend too long on the 3-mark questions – put your answer in bullet points if you are struggling for time.

AO1: Part (a) of this question asks you to show knowledge and understanding of specific content from a religion by responding to a question that follows a short text related to that religion.

EXPLAIN

Provide a detailed description or summary with reasons or causes.

Try to think of about six points as to how a Taoist connects with 'The Profound Mystery'. Write down all you know and expand on your answer from there.

AO2: Part (b) of this question asks you to show your understanding by applying your content knowledge as it relates to the text and to analyse how that information connects to the essential questions for that religion.

Jainism

Study the passage below and answer the questions which follow.

8. 'All breathing, existing, living, sentient creatures should not be slain, nor treated with violence, nor abused, nor tormented, nor driven away.

    This is the pure, unchangeable, eternal law, which the clever ones, who understand the world, have declared… "that is the truth, that is so, that is proclaimed in this (creed)".

    Having adopted (the law), one should not hide it, nor forsake it. Correctly understanding the law, one should arrive at indifference for the impressions of the senses, and "not act on the motives of the world". "He who is not of this mind, how should he come to the other?"'

Jaina Sutras

(a) Identify **three** teachings in this passage. [3]

(b) Explain the role of non-violence in Jainism. [6]

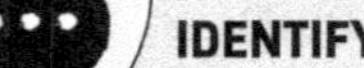

IDENTIFY

Write an answer from multiple possibilities.

Remember to use religious vocabulary in your answers.

Make sure that you focus on non-injury in Jainism, rather than discussing how that concept relates to other religions such as Hinduism.

It is important to think through distinctions between Jainism and Hinduism so that you clearly focus on the religion that the question is discussing. Some terminology and concepts are quite similar.

EXPLAIN

Provide a detailed description or summary with reasons or causes.

Consider all the different meanings and connotations of 'non-violence'. How does it play a role?

You may want to write down all of the terminology that you know about Jainism and determine which words would be relevant to the passage and to non-violence.

Remember that non-violence can be about interactions with people in addition to rules about foods that should not be eaten.

Bahá'i Faith

Study the passage below and answer the questions which follow.

9. 'Be generous in prosperity and thankful in adversity,
    Be fair in thy judgment, and guarded in thy speech.
    Be a lamp unto those who walk in darkness, and a home to the stranger.
    Be eyes to the blind, and a guiding light unto the feet of the erring.
    Be a breath of life to the body of humankind, a dew to the soil of the human heart,
    and a fruit upon the tree of humility.'

    Bahá'u'lláh

(a) Identify **three** teachings about ethics in this passage. **[3]**

(b) Explain Bahá'i beliefs on ethics. **[6]**

IDENTIFY

Write an answer from multiple possibilities.

Use the passage to support your answer.

You have more than three options to identify for teachings, so make sure to include specific vocabulary and be specific for each teaching.

AO1: Part (a) of this question asks you to show knowledge and understanding of specific content from a religion by responding to a question that follows a short text related to that religion.

EXPLAIN

Provide a detailed description or summary with reasons or causes.

Ethics is a very large topic, so just pick out a couple of points and expand on these to make a well-rounded, informed answer.

Because so much of the Bahá'i Faith is based on ethics, you may want to write the key content and terminology that you know and decide how well your knowledge relates to the question and the passage.

AO2: Part (b) of this question asks you to show your understanding by applying your content knowledge as it relates to the text and to analyse how that information connects to the essential questions for that religion.

Set B

Paper 2

Set your timer for 1 hour 30 minutes.

You will choose one question from Section A and one question from Section B.
Each question is worth 15 marks.

There is space under each question option to write a short plan and to make a note of
the key terms and things to remember.

Once you have made your choice, you can find the spaces to write your answer on page 71
for your Section A question and page 79 for your Section B question.

Section A

Answer **one** question from this section.

Hinduism

1. Discuss the connection between Varna and Dharma in Hinduism.　　**[15]**

2. Discuss to what extent Raja Yoga is the most appropriate yogic path
for a Hindu.　　**[15]**

Plan your answer in these boxes

Remember to given an even-handed response that covers all components of the question with the command term 'discuss'. In this case, be sure to discuss Varna, Dharma and the ways in which they connect to a Hindu practitioner's life.

Do not confuse Varna with Ashrama. However, a thorough response will also discuss Ashrama, or the phase of a practitioner's life, in connection to Varna.

Be sure to define the terminology at some point in your answer, either in the introduction or in the paragraphs you plan on writing about each concept. Do not assume the reader understands the definition, and be sure to clearly explain it for them.

When discussing the extent to which Raja Yoga is the most 'appropriate' path, be sure to include the other major yogic paths somewhere within your response (Karma, Bhatki, and Jnana). However, most of your response should focus on the Raja Yogic path.

TO WHAT EXTENT

This usually means you need to provide an evaluative component to your
response which measures the main factor of the question against others. In this
case, you should measure Raja against the other three main paths.

Buddhism

3. Compare and contrast the ways in which Mahayana and Theravada practitioners interpret and apply the life of Siddhartha Guatama to their own lives and teachings. **[15]**

COMPARE AND CONTRAST

Write a response about the similarities and differences between two or more concepts or terms, making sure to address both throughout.

In this case, consider the commonalities that exist between Mahayana and Theravada belief systems. Examples could be emphasized doctrine, reverence to Siddhartha Guatama's life, or practice. Be sure to thoughtfully explain and describe where the schools of thought diverge.

4. The Dalai Lama has stated that 'Everything is interconnected'. Using your knowledge of the role tanha and dukkha play in a practitioner's everyday life, discuss the extent to which you agree with this statement. **[15]**

DISCUSS

Write a detailed response that considers a range of perspectives, arguments, and factors with conclusions supported with evidence.

This prompt is asking you to weigh up the extent to which you agree with the Dalai Lama. Be sure to explain who he is and what his role is in Buddhism before you justify your argument. Always explain or describe the factor that is mentioned in the question before you offer your opinion.

Sikhism

5. Examine the role of salvation in Sikhism through doctrine and teachings. **[15]**

EXAMINE

Determine the nature of a concept or claim in detail.

Can you recognize the Sanskrit references to world religions vocabulary? They won't always be defined for you in the exam. Here, you must recognize that 'Tanha' means cravings or desire and 'Dukkha' means suffering.

Make sure to define mukti: liberation in Sikhism is reaching a union with God and being freed from the cycle of rebirth.

The concept of salvation is present in many religions. Remember to answer only about salvation in Sikhism.

6. Compare and contrast the philosophies and teachings of two of the major Sikh gurus. **[15]**

COMPARE AND CONTRAST

Write a response about the similarities and differences between two or more concepts or terms, making sure to address both throughout.

You may want to start with Guru Nanak, the founder of Sikhism, and discuss the foundation beliefs of the religion. For your second guru, consider the changes and developments that have occurred in Sikhism.

Remember to include your religious vocabulary specific to Sikhism.

Open-ended question

7. Examine the role and interpretations of God in **either** Hinduism, Buddhism **or** Sikhism. **[15]**

Answer lines for Set B Paper 2 (Section A)

NOTES

NOTES

NOTES

NOTES

Section B

Answer **one** question from this section.

Judaism

8. 'That which is despicable to you, do not do to your fellow, this is the whole Torah, and the rest is commentary, go and learn it.'

Rabbi Hillel, Babylonian Talmud, Shabbat 31a

To what extent do you agree with this statement? **[15]**

9. Examine the nature of *tikkun olam* in Judaism. **[15]**

Plan your answer in these boxes

TO WHAT EXTENT

Write a detailed response with multiple arguments and consider the strengths and weaknesses of each argument.

Start by breaking down the quote. Rabbi Hillel is stating that being good to other people is at the heart of everything in the Torah.

Consider differences among the movements of Judaism to help structure your response.

You may want to review the establishment of the Torah and provide a brief overview of what it discusses.

Do not base your answer on insider or outsider perspectives.

EXAMINE

Determine the nature of a concept or claim in detail.

This question asks you to discuss a very specific vocabulary word that can connect to other content. If you aren't sure of the word, that's okay! The best strategy is to read through other questions and find one that you are sure you can answer.

Start by defining the term *tikkun olam* and what it means to Jewish practitioners.

Focus on ethical decisions that Jewish practitioners make. You may want to discuss why Judaism believes that it is necessary to repair the world.

Christianity

10. Discuss original sin in Christianity.   [15]

Write a detailed response that considers a range of perspectives, arguments and factors, with conclusions supported with evidence.

Start by defining original sin and make sure to distinguish it from actual individual sins that humans commit.

It would be useful to reference the banishment of Adam and Eve from the Garden of Eden in Genesis, the first book of the Old Testament of the Christian Bible.

11. Discuss how salvation is achieved in Christianity.   [15]

DISCUSS

Write a detailed response that considers a range of perspectives, arguments, and factors with conclusions supported with evidence.

It is not necessary to memorize verses from the Christian Bible to prepare for these questions, but it is useful to review some of the significant teachings from the Old and New Testaments.

Start by defining salvation in Christianity and Christian beliefs regarding the afterlife.

Continue your response by discussing ways that Christian practitioners can lead a good life according to Christian doctrine.

This question is similar to the IB guiding questions for each religion: 'Where are we going?' and 'How do we get there?'

Salvation is a concept that has different meanings in other religions. Make sure that you are clear on the meaning for Christianity.

Islam

12. Examine the role of women in Islam. [15]

13. Discuss the nature of Allah in Islam. [15]

Open-ended question

14. With reference to **one** religion, **either** Judaism **or** Christianity **or** Islam, discuss the beliefs regarding eschatology. **[15]**

Answer lines for Set B Paper 2 (Section B)

DISCUSS

Write a detailed response that considers a range of perspectives, arguments and factors, with conclusions supported with evidence.

Demonstrate that you know what eschatology means by defining it more generally before discussing it for one of the religions. (It is the part of a religion that focuses on death and the afterlife.)

There are similarities and differences in eschatology in the three Abrahamic religions (Judaism, Christianity, and Islam). Make sure you choose the religion you have studied in depth.

Only discuss one religion. You will not get extra marks by discussing more than one or comparing the religions.

If you are a practitioner of a specific religion, it may be tempting to write about that religion. Make sure to answer questions based on your academic study of the religion, rather than basing your information on your practice of the religion.

NOTES

NOTES

NOTES

NOTES

Set C

This set of papers has no additional help in the margins. There is a space to write notes so you can plan what you are going to write if needed.

Paper 1

Set your timer for 1 hour 15 minutes.

Answer a total of **five** questions, selecting **at least one** from **each** section (A, B and C).

Section A

Make sure at least one of your five questions is from Section A.

Hinduism

Study the passage below and answer the questions which follow.

1. 'And he who sees everything in his atman, and his atman in everything, does not seek to hide himself from that, in whom all beings have become one with his own atman. What perplexity, what sorrow, is there when he sees this oneness? He [the self] pervades all, resplendent, bodiless, woundless, without muscles, pure, untouched by evil; far-seeing, transcendent, self-being, disposing ends through perpetual ages.'

    Isha Upanishad, Hymns 6–8

    (a) Identify **three** teachings in this passage. **[3]**

    (b) Explain Hindu beliefs about atman and Brahman. **[6]**

NOTES

Buddhism

Study the passage below and answer the questions which follow.

2. 'People followed by thirst [tanha] crawl around like a captured hare. Therefore, you should remove thirst and wish for being free of passions yourselves.'

Dhammapada 343

(a) Identify **three** teachings in this passage. [3]

(b) Explain what role tanha or thirst has in Buddhist beliefs. [6]

NOTES

Sikhism

Study the passage below and answer the questions which follow.

3. 'There is One Creator; Eternal truth is its name;
    Creator of all things, Fearing nothing and at enmity with no one,
    Timeless being; Beyond birth and death;
    Self-existent; By the grace of the Guru, made known to human beings.'

Guru Granth Sahib 1

(a) Identify **three** teachings in this passage.   [3]

(b) Explain the importance of the guru in Sikhism.   [6]

Section B

Make sure at least one of your five questions is from Section B.

Judaism

Study the passage below and answer the questions which follow.

4. 'Hear, O Israel: The Lord is our God, the Lord is one. You shall love the Lord your God with all your heart, and with all your soul, and with all your might. Keep these words that I am commanding you today in your heart.'

Deuteronomy 6:2–4

(a) Identify **three** teachings in this passage. **[3]**

(b) Explain the importance of the Shema in Judaism. **[6]**

Christianity

Study the passage below and answer the questions which follow.

5. 'But if we walk in the light, as he is in the light, we have fellowship with one another, and the blood of Jesus, his Son, purifies us from all sin. If we claim to be without sin, we deceive ourselves and the truth is not in us. If we confess our sins, he is faithful and just and will forgive us our sins and purify us from all unrighteousness.

1 John 1:7–9

(a) Identify **three** teachings in this passage. [3]

(b) Explain Christian beliefs about sin. [6]

NOTES

Islam

Study the passage below and answer the questions which follow.

6. 'Every soul shall have a taste of death: And only on the Day of Judgment shall you be paid your full recompense. Only he who is saved far from the Fire and admitted to the Garden will have attained the object (of Life): For the life of this world is but goods and chattels of deception.'

Surah 3:185

(a) Identify **three** teachings in this passage. [3]

(b) Explain Muslim beliefs about life after death. [6]

NOTES

Section C

NOTES

Make sure at least one of your five questions is from Section C.

Taoism

Study the passage below and answer the questions which follow.

7. 'The Dao does nothing, but leaves nothing undone.
If the powerful men could observe it, all creations would be transformed by themselves.'

Lao Tzu, Tao Te Cheng

(a) Identify **three** teachings in this passage. [3]

(b) Explain Daoist beliefs about the doctrine of wu wei or non-action. [6]

Jainism

Study the passage below and answer the questions which follow.

8. 'The molecules are capable of being transformed into karma as a result of the thought activity of the jiva, yet this transformation is not caused by jiva itself.'

   (a) Identify **three** teachings in this passage. [3]

   (b) Explain Jain teaching about karma. [6]

NOTES

Bahá'i Faith

Study the passage below and answer the questions which follow.

9. 'Know thou that every soul is fashioned after the nature of God, each being
    pure and holy at his birth. Afterwards, however, the individuals will vary
    according to what they acquire of virtues or vices in this world…'

Abdu'l-Baha

(a) Identify **three** teachings in this passage.   [3]

(b) Explain Bahá'i beliefs about the human condition.   [6]

NOTES

Set C
Paper 2

Set your timer for 1 hour 30 minutes.

Each question is worth 15 marks.

There is space under each question option to write a short plan and to make a note of the key terms and things to remember.

Once you have made your choice, you can find the space to write your answers on page 96 for your Section A question and page 104 for your Section B question.

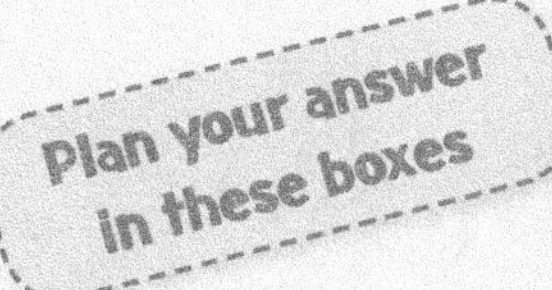

Section A

Answer **one** question from this section.

Hinduism

1. 'Hinduism is a non-violent tradition'. Discuss. **[15]**

2. 'The Vedas are irrelevant and inaccessible to most Hindus.' To what extent do you agree with this statement? **[15]**

NOTES

Buddhism

3. Discuss the importance of the Four Noble Truths in Buddhism. **[15]**

4. Analyse the importance of meditation in Buddhism. **[15]**

NOTES

5. 'The Guru Granth Sahib is the only important Sikh sacred text.' Discuss. **[15]**

6. To what extent are teachings of equality applied in Sikh communities? **[15]**

NOTES

Open-ended question

7. With reference to **one** religion, **either** Hinduism **or** Buddhism **or** Sikhism, discuss views on divorce. **[15]**

Answer lines for Set C Paper 2 (Section A)

NOTES

NOTES

NOTES

NOTES

Continue on to another piece of paper if you need to...

Section B

Answer **one** question from this section.

Judaism

8. 'The Torah is the most important Jewish sacred text.' Discuss.   [15]

9. Examine the importance of the Sabbath in Jewish belief and practice.   [15]

NOTES

Christianity

10. Discuss Christian beliefs about baptism. [15]

11. 'Christianity teaches pacifism.' Examine this claim. [15]

NOTES

12. Examine the basis for the authority of the Qur'an and the Hadith. **[15]**

13. 'Al Fatiha* is the single most important surah in the Qur'an.' Discuss. **[15]**

*the first chapter of the Qur'an

Open-ended question

14. With reference to **one** religion, **either** Judaism **or** Christianity **or** Islam, discuss various views on abortion. **[15]**

Answer lines for Set C Paper 2 (Section B)

NOTES

NOTES

NOTES

Answers

Set A

Paper 1: Section A

1. (a)
- One belief shown in the passage is the presence of the Hindu Trimurti, that contains Shiva, Vishnu and Brahma (the creative, destructive, and preservationist force of Brahman)
- Another belief is that of the cyclical universe, in which all things in the universe will go through periods of creation and destruction, similar to the life of a Hindu practitioner throughout the cycle of birth and rebirth with samsara
- The nature of the God-force in Hinduism (Brahman) is limitless and all encompassing **[3 marks]**

(b)
- Brahman manifests in various forms for Hindu practitioners. Those of 'lower' nature are envisioned in tangible ways that a Hindu practitioner can connect and relate to, or use for worship
- One such way is through the murti, or windows into the divine, of Brahman. Murti exist in various lower nature God forms, such as Ganesh or Durga, and are represented in paintings or sculpture
- Another way in which Brahman's lower nature is manifested is through avatars (human incarnations of Brahman). Of these, the most well known is Krishna in the Bhagavad Gita
- These forms exist to communicate Brahman's all-encompassing power, and so that Hindu practitioners can connect to that power and uncover their atman (soul in connection to Brahman)
- Brahman's 'higher nature' is that which is eternal and all-encompassing. Monism, meaning that everything can be traced back to a single source, is related to Brahman's higher nature, which is prevalent in everything
- This higher nature is responsible for the creation, upkeep, and destruction of the world, and also the existence of all beings that make up this world and multiple universes outside of it **[6 marks]**

2. (a)
- One belief present in the passage that represents craving (desire) is *tanha*, which is represented by greed and false hopes
- Another belief present in the passage is samsara (the continuous cycle of birth and rebirth), represented by 'over and over again they are born'
- An additional belief present in the passage is the concept of attachment, which manifests negatively in the form of cravings, and keeps a practitioner within the cycle of samsara **[3 marks]**

(b)
- It is not until a Buddhist practitioner is able to overcome their tanha (desires) that they will be able to escape the continuous cycle of birth and rebirth, also known as samsara
- Because individuals are attached to cravings and desire, it takes great work to understand that these attachments must be broken in order to eventually achieve nirvana, or the escape from the cycle of samsara
- Attachments to desires and cravings actually cause suffering. Once a Buddhist practitioner realizes dukkha (that life is suffering), they understand the first step of the Four Noble Truths, and are able to embark upon the path of releasing themselves from this suffering and achieving nirvana
- The second of the Four Noble Truths is that suffering is caused by attachment and cravings. Practitioners must understand how these attachments manifest in their daily lives in order to overcome them
- The Third Noble Truth is the understanding that although life is suffering because of desires and cravings, there is a way to overcome them
- 'The Way' to overcome desires and cravings is the Fourth Noble Truth, which is also in the Eightfold Path, a set of eight steps needed to achieve nirvana. Following this path will release a practitioner from tanha and dukkha and allow them to reach nirvana **[6 marks]**

3. (a)
- Although maya (worldly illusions) attempt to pull humans away from God, the Eternal Being is the permanent truth, which is referenced in the phrase 'death shall not approach You', as God is never ending
- 'The impure, the stupid and the foolish' is a reference to those who have given in to haumai (self-centeredness or ego). This self-centeredness gets in the way of being closer to realizing God and it can be overcome by sewa (selflessness)
- 'You are present within all, You are above all' is a reference to both the monotheism of Sikhism and the concept that there is divinity within each person **[3 marks]**

(b)
- The human condition is one that is often focused on being manmukh, or following one's ego and giving in to the baser desires and having no regard for other people
- People who are manmukh give into the five vices: lust, covetousness, attachment, anger and pride
- Practitioners must work to overcome manmukh and be gurmukh, which means to live a God-centred way of life that is in accordance with the teachings of the gurus
- Humans spend their lives in a cycle of birth and rebirth, with the final goal being to reach mukti, liberation, and be in union with God
- Sikh practitioners have the capability of leading a life that brings them closer to God. By following the teachings of the gurus and serving others (sewa), humans can become closer to a union with God
- Sikh practitioners should follow the three duties: nam jampo (remembering God's name); kirat karni (earning an honest living) and vand ke chakna (giving to charity)
- These duties guide Sikh practitioners along with the teachings of the gurus to live according to God's will by doing good deeds and meditating on God **[6 marks]**

Paper 1: Section B

4. (a)
- A Jewish practitioner should receive a punishment appropriate to the 'injury' or wrongdoing they committed
- Disputes regarding the law can be held in Beth Din (Jewish rabbinical courts) to determine the appropriate punishment
- Referring to 'neighbour' Jewish practitioners should apply this rule to 'injury' against all people, not just other Jewish practitioners **[3 marks]**

(b)
- Jewish practitioners adhere to the Halakhah (collection of Jewish laws from the written and oral Torah) as it is central to living a life according to the will of God
- The Decalogue (the Ten Commandments given to Moses on Mt. Sinai) is extremely important in the lives of Jewish practitioners and it provides guidance for living a good life on a daily basis
- The 613 mitzvot are commandments found in the Torah that Jewish practitioners are expected to follow
- There are debates in the different movements of Judaism (Orthodox, Conservative, and Reform) about the extent to which practitioners are expected to follow the 613 mitzvot and the Torah in a modern society
- For some practitioners, adhering to Jewish law in their daily lives is a way of showing their devotion to God
- For some practitioners, adhering to Jewish law ensures that they are following the goals of Judaism to repair the world (tikkun olam) in preparation for the world to come **[6 marks]**

5. (a)
- Love is central to the Christian religion and to the teachings of Jesus
- Christianity emphasizes love for other humans and the need to love God to reach the Kingdom of Heaven
- All other aspects of life, here 'clanging cymbals', are distractions from the importance of loving God and loving one another **[3 marks]**

(b)
- Christian practitioners should practice agape which is the highest form of love and charity
- Christian practitioners are blessed with God's grace – unmerited, unconditional love from God
- The goal in Christianity is to reach the Kingdom of Heaven, a place with no suffering and an eternal union with God
- Christian practitioners should believe in the Trinity (God the Father, God the Son, and God the Holy Spirit) and adhere to the teachings of Jesus in the Christian Bible to reach the Kingdom of Heaven

- Despite being marked by original sin (the sin described in the story of Adam and Eve in Genesis of the Christian Bible) Christian practitioners can still reach the Kingdom of Heaven because of God's grace
- Christian practitioners can partake in the sacraments, which are rituals that can be traced to acts of Jesus, and thereby show their love of God
- The way that sacraments are practiced may vary by denomination and may vary in significance by denomination **[6 marks]**

6. (a)
- The concept of tawhid (the unique oneness of Allah)
- Allah is all-knowing both on earth and in the afterlife
- There will be a Day of Judgement for Muslims based on the deeds they did on earth **[3 marks]**

(b)
- The above passage refers to leading a righteous life as a practitioner of Islam by submitting to the will of Allah (the divine being of Islam)
- The will of Allah was revealed to the prophet Muhammad (PBUH) and set forth in the Qur'an (the sacred text of Islam)
- The Day of Judgement will determine where Muslims will go in the afterlife
- The goal is to reach Janna (the heaven which is described as a garden paradise)
- Those who have not lived a righteous life will go to Jahannam (hellfire) a place of eternal suffering
- Muslims can live by the Five Pillars of Islam: faith in Allah, prayers, charity, fasting, and pilgrimage, which are listed in the Hadith (sacred text of the teachings and actions of the prophet Muhammad (PBUH)) **[6 marks]**

Paper 1: Section C

7. (a)
- Wu wei (effortless action or action without forced control) is present in relation to 'going against the Tao'
- Fu is symbolically represented in the passage, as referenced with the sage 'moving through life not caring about home or name' as they understand that through fu, all things will return back to their source.
- An additional belief represented in the passage is the ideal in which a practitioner will live in harmony or in accordance with the Tao (the underlying set of principles or force that sustains the world) **[3 marks]**

(b)
- Ultimately, the major goal of Taoism is for a practitioner to live in harmony and balance with the Tao that, although it goes unnamed, is the life force of the universe
- One way in which a practitioner can achieve this balance is through maintaining yin-yang (the balancing of opposite or contrary forces) as interconnected and complementary to one another
- Maintaining the balance of one's chi (individual life force energy) is necessary if one is to live in harmony with the Tao
- A way in which a practitioner can maintain and harness one's chi is through various physical and mental exercises such as tai chi, in which a practitioner undertakes ancient meditative movements
- Meditative movements in tai chi aid a practitioner in maintaining their breath and practising Qigong (meditative breath skill) in order to maintain energy flow within the body and live harmoniously outwardly
- Meditative movements and deliberate action allow a practitioner to maintain the three purities or three vehicles. The three purities are creative energy, life force energy, and spiritual energy, and they further allow a practitioner to live according to the Tao, or in harmony with it **[6 marks]**

8. (a)
- Ahimsa (non-violence) is to be observed to both humans and animals
- The right actions that a Jain practitioner observes will impact their rebirth as determined by karma
- Harm done to others impacts one's self, as a Jain practitioner could be reborn as a human or an animal **[3 marks]**

(b)
- To achieve the goals of Jainism, practitioners follow the Five Great Vows
- The Five Great Vows are: non-violence, truth, non-stealing, celibacy, and non-attachment
- The most important of the Five Great Vows in Jainism is ahimsa
- Jain practitioners should have right knowledge, right faith, and right conduct to achieve the goal of liberation

- Jain practitioners can achieve the goal of liberation (moksha)
- Jain practitioners will continue to be reborn, and that rebirth is determined by karma, until they are liberated
- All actions, thoughts, words, and deeds have an effect (karma) and karma sticks to the soul (jiva)
- With effort and discipline, Jain practitioners can control karma and eventually be liberated
- Once the jiva is freed from the ajiva (the karma that weighs down the jiva), the soul will no longer be reborn (thus ending the cycle of samsara) and instead will exist in a state of all-knowing bliss
- In order to break the cycle of samsara, beings must avoid selfish or harmful actions, and must engage in suffering to lighten the karma of the soul. **[6 marks]**

9. (a)
- 'The fruits of one tree' is a reference to the unity of all religions in Bahá'í
- 'Harmony' relates to the belief in accepting the validity of all religions in Bahá'í
- The 'illumination' can relate to the many messengers and manifestations of God **[3 marks]**

(b)
- Unity is central to Bahá'í – people of all religious traditions can work together to benefit society
- Bahá'í practitioners believe in the validity of the origins of all religions, which supports the concept of unity of all people
- Bahá'í practitioners acknowledge the prophets of other religions (Moses, Muhammad (PBUH), and Jesus) as being messengers of God and there is unity in those messengers
- Bahá'í practitioners believe in the unity of all people as being from a single race, and in the equality of the sexes
- Bahá'í practitioners believe that there is unity in diversity and that cultural and ethnic diversity is necessary for the development of humans
- Bahá'í practitioners are expected to follow the teachings of Bahá'u'lláh, and the most important teaching is of unity **[6 marks]**

SET A

Paper 2: Section A

1.
- Darshan is the act of seeing and being seen by the divine (Brahman) and usually relates to the way in which a Hindu practitioner chooses to connect with God
- Murti is a window or a means of communication with the divine (Brahman) which can take various forms
- The most common forms of murti are sculptures, paintings or other physical manifestation of the divine. Whatever the form of murti might be, it is used to cultivate a relationship with Brahman and to allow a practitioner to personally connect to the God-force in Hinduism
- However, other mechanisms exist to aid Hindu practitioners in achieving darshan, and these mechanisms are largely based on practitioners' personality types and what will be a good fit for them
- Some practitioners might choose to work towards the feeling of darshan by being outdoors and one with nature, where they can connect with God without interference from individuals or material items that they might deem distracting
- Other practitioners might choose to learn from a priest or guru to cultivate their understanding of Hindu concepts (such as yoga or various pieces of doctrine), in order to better understand the nature of God
- The mechanism one uses to connect with God depends on many factors, such as geography, family origin, personality and personal choice. Because Hinduism is a pluralistic religion, multiple paths can be pursued by the practitioner in order to achieve darshan **[15 marks]**

2.
- Moksha (or the release from the endless cycle of birth and rebirth in samsara) is the major goal of most Hindu practitioners
- However, there are many additional goals that a practitioner must work toward and achieve more immediately before moksha is achieved, as this final release is believed to take multiple lifetimes
- Earning good karma and performing karmic deeds in this lifetime is necessary to elevate one's standing in the next lifetime. The choice to act in ways to attain good karma allows a practitioner free will and to determine aspects of their future life paths
- Working toward fulfilling one's dharma (one's duty to society and moral law in accordance to their lives)

- Dharma and karma act in cooperation to affect a practitioner's next stage in samsara
- A practitioner's varna (or social group and occupation) is determined based on personality and nature. Whatever occupation a practitioner enters, they are expected to uphold their personal duty to their work in order to contribute to a well-functioning society
- Lastly, ashrama refers to a practitioner's life stage in Hindu society, which spans from being a student to retirement. It is expected that at various points in a practitioner's life, they are carrying out duties that are appropriate for their age and obligations
- Therefore, while moksha is the primary goal, other preliminary and more immediate goals exist that a practitioner must meet in order to eventually achieve moksha **[15 marks]**

3.
- The sangha (monastic community) is one of the three jewels in Buddhist worship and practice
- The Three Jewels (or cornerstones of Buddhism) are the sangha, dhamma and Buddha. The Buddha refers to the original founder of Buddhism (Siddhartha Guatama) and the dhamma refers to the word of the Buddha (Buddhist doctrine)
- Siddhartha Guatama is considered to be the founder of Buddhism: the revered individual who became enlightened under the Bodhi Tree and eventually achieved nirvana (or escape from samsara, the cycle of rebirth)
- Guatama put forth various pieces of doctrine (dhamma) that Buddhist practitioners were to adhere to if they too wanted to reach enlightenment. Examples of the dhamma are the Four Noble Truths and the Eightfold Path
- The sangha plays an integral role in Buddhist worship and teachings because this is the part of the Buddhist community that is responsible for interpreting and relaying the teachings of Siddhartha
- Depending on the Buddhist sect, members of the sangha might interpret various portions of the dhamma differently:
  - Mahayana Buddhists might emphasize the portion of the Buddha's life in which he returned from his enlightened state to help members of the public achieve nirvana
  - Theravada Buddhists might emphasize the point of Buddha's life in which he realized life was suffering, according to the first of the Four Noble Truths, and that the way to alleviate it is through the Fourth Noble Truth, or the Eightfold Path
- The sangha also plays an integral role in Buddhist worship and teachings because it provides a common place for practitioners to worship, maintaining temples and helping to spread the word of Siddhartha amongst the community
- The sangha acts in conjunction with the dhamma and the Buddha, as one cornerstone cannot fully exist without another portion of the three jewels **[15 marks]**

4.
- There are some Buddhist beliefs that are uniform no matter the sect or geographic area in which a practitioner lives. Some of these beliefs are adherence to the Three Jewels (the Buddha, the Sangha and the Dhamma) and different forms of doctrine, such as the Four Noble Truths, the Eightfold Path and the Precepts
- All Buddhists revere, in some way, the life of Siddhartha Guatama (Buddhism's original founder). Some interpret his role as being that of an original sage, while others believe him to be one of many holy individuals in the Buddhist tradition
- Theravada and Mahayana schools of thought are similar to a moderate extent, as they both revere the life of Siddhartha and adhere to similar pieces of doctrine; however, they differ in their beliefs regarding which part of Siddhartha's life they allow to guide their beliefs and practice
- Theravada Buddhists emphasize the portion of Siddhartha's life in which he sat beneath the Bodhi Tree and initially attained enlightenment. Therefore, they emphasize inner wisdom and intellectualism as the primary route that will allow a practitioner to reach enlightenment
- Mahayana Buddhists emphasize the portion of Siddhartha's life in which he was on the verge of giving up on his meditation practice, after he renounced the world and material possessions. A woman came to him and offered him a bowl of rice and this act, to Mahayana Buddhists, is the act of compassion that allowed Siddhartha to eventually attain enlightenment. Therefore, compassion and community is what is emphasized in Mahayana Buddhism
- Holy individuals who came after Siddhartha Guatama in Theravada Buddhism are called arhats, while in Mahayana Buddhism they are called Boddhisattvas. In Mahayana Buddhism, a Boddhisattva might be revered in the same way Siddhartha is, with their words being considered sacred and worthy of worship. An arhat is revered, but Siddhartha Guatama's words and actions take precedence

- While both schools of thought are similar in their foundational beliefs, they differ in the portions of Siddhartha Guatama's life that guide their practice, and in the way in which they emphasize actions with other members of the community on the road to enlightenment **[15 marks]**

5.
- Guru Nanak established the foundational beliefs of Sikhism: that God is transcendent and that God is one, which distinguishes Sikhism as being monotheistic
- Guru Nanak also taught that every human can have direct access to God, and that there is no need for formal rituals or interventions from religious leaders in order to access God. Guru Nanak emphasized the divinity within all humans regardless of their background
- Guru Nanak's belief in the direct access to God had significant social implications, as he denounced the caste system in India in the 15th century and also established gender equality within the religion
- Guru Nanak also promoted the foundational belief that the way to a spiritual existence is through meditation on God's name (nam japna) and doing good deeds, and these beliefs are fundamental to the practise of Sikhism
- However, it is important to consider the significance of Sri Guru Granth Sahib (the 'Eternal Guru of the Sikhs'). Sri Guru Granth Sahib is the sacred text of Sikhism, containing poetry of the Gurus as well as writings from other religions that were consistent with beliefs in Sikhism
- Sri Guru Granth Sahib is not only the Sikh scripture, but is also considered the last and final 'eternal living guru' which shows its authority within Sikhism
- One must also consider the beliefs of Guru Gobind Singh (the last of the ten gurus) as having a transformative impact on the lives and beliefs of Sikh practitioners
- Guru Gobind Singh created the Khalsa, a community of devoted practitioners who wore visible symbols of their faith, including the turban for men
- He also established the festival day of Vaisakhi (transforming the order into soldier-saints) and the Amrit initiation ceremony through which Sikhs become fully initiated practitioners
- Initiates take new names and wear the five Ks, the physical symbols that visibly distinguish individuals as Sikh practitioners
- Perhaps the most significant contribution to the beliefs and lives of Sikh practitioners was Guru Gobind Singh's declaration of the scripture Sri Guru Granth Sahib as the next guru, rather than a human, establishing it as the 'Eternal Guru of the Sikhs' **[15 marks]**

6.
- The sacred scripture of Sikhism is Sri Guru Granth Sahib, which is so sacred and significant in the lives of Sikh practitioners that it was also declared a guru by Guru Gobind Singh and it is known as the 'Eternal Guru of the Sikhs'
- As Sikhism is about doing good deeds (sewa) as well as meditating on God's name (nam japna) these extend to the social and political lives of Sikh practitioners and were codified in the scripture Sri Guru Granth Sahib
- Central to Sikhism are the three duties that practitioners should follow: nam jampo (remembering God's name), kirat karni (earning an honest living) and vand ke chakna (giving to charity)
- The Panth (global community of Sikh practitioners) focuses on the political and social concerns of justice and charity, and many practitioners share langar (a free meal available to everyone) in order to promote social justice and remain gurmukh (living a God-centered way of life that is in accordance with the gurus)
- On the establishment of Sikhism in the 15th century by Guru Nanak, he denounced hierarchies including the caste system and all forms of inequality, declaring that differences in gender, social class or religion did not matter. He included in the Sikh scripture that everyone has jot (divinity within) and that everyone can reach a union with God. These beliefs have a significant impact on the social and political lives of Sikh practitioners **[15 marks]**

7.
- The afterlife affects Buddhist practitioners in various ways, though the afterlife itself is not defined in concrete terms unlike in Abrahamic faiths
- There are two interpretations of the afterlife in Buddhism:
  - one: the immediate life that comes after this worldly life
  - two: the afterlife that comes when one has escaped the cycle of samsara (rebirth) and has reached nirvana
- The immediate afterlife (or next life in the cycle of samsara) affects a Buddhist practitioner on a daily basis, as they worship and exist throughout the world. If a practitioner follows the dhamma (word of the Buddha) and adheres to doctrine (such

as the Precepts and Four Noble Truths), then they may begin to elevate themselves in the next life
- Throughout the cycle of samsara, a Buddhist practitioner will acquire more knowledge and awareness so that eventually they will reach enlightenment and nirvana (escape from the cycle of samsara)
- The eventual afterlife, when a practitioner has escaped the suffering of this world, is undefined in Buddhism. Buddhist doctrine does not confirm or deny the existence of a God, and refrains from describing the afterlife
- We do understand, though, that reaching this afterlife and achieving nirvana is the end goal for all Buddhist practitioners. While this is the long-term goal, more immediate goals of adherence to various forms of doctrine and conducting life in accordance with compassion and wisdom guide an individual on a daily basis

[15 marks]

Paper 2: Section B

8.
- Kosher laws are kashrut (dietary laws) that are important to the daily practice of Judaism for many practitioners
- Kosher laws are connected to 613 mitvot in Judaism as set forth in the Torah
- The extent to which practitioners adhere to kosher food laws often depends upon their movement within Judaism: Orthodox, Conservative or Reform, with Orthodox Jews following the literal interpretation of the law
- A Jewish practitioner is considered to have transgressed even if they were unaware that they were breaking a kosher law
- Kosher food laws have both health and ethical implications as outlined in detail in the book of Leviticus
- One ethical implication is that animals who are slaughtered for food should feel no pain. Even though God gives man dominion over animals according to the book of Genesis, they are also creatures of God and should not experience pain
- One health implication is that animals that were not killed for food and died from other causes should not be eaten. They were not slaughtered in a proper way which is not kosher and has the potential to cause sickness **[15 marks]**

9.
- The Bar Mitzvah (Bat Mitzvah for females) is a rite of passage (an event that celebrates a significant moment in a person's life) in which a practitioner gains the responsibility of an adult in the Jewish community
- The ritual involves the transition of an adolescent (age 13 for boys and age 12 for girls) from having yetzer hara (evil inclination, often understood as selfish inclination) to having yetzer hatov (good inclination)
- The increased responsibility gained on completing a Bar/Bat Mitzvah means that the individual can be called up to read from the Torah (aliyah) at the bimah (raised platform in a synagogue where the Torah is read) during a service
- The individual can also be called upon to be a part of a minyan (a quorum of 10 Jewish practitioners needed for a prayer service)
- The Jewish community supports the individual as they prepare for a Bar/Bar Mitzvah. The preparation can take approximately a year, to prepare to read in Hebrew from the Torah in front of the religious community of family and friends, and it is a celebratory occasion
- The Bar/Bar Mitzvah is significant for the worldwide Jewish diaspora as one of the goals of Judaism is the preservation of the religion **[15 marks]**

10.
- Sacraments are sacred rituals (outward acts to show a practitioner's devotion to God) that are from Jesus to give grace (God's unmerited, unconditional love)
- Each of the seven sacraments can be traced to an action done by Jesus
- Sacraments can be divided into three categories: sacraments of initiation, healing and vocation
- Sacraments of initiation are baptism, confirmation and the Eucharist (these are initiation rituals because they bring the practitioners into the Christian community)
- Sacraments of healing are anointing the sick and reconciliation (Anointing the sick helps to heal the body, and reconciliation helps to heal the practitioner's relationship with God)
- Sacraments of vocation are matrimony or taking holy orders (these sacraments affirm the life that God chose for His people and are considered callings)

- Sacraments may differ in practice and significance, or may not be a part of Protestant denominations (belonging instead only to Catholicism). For example, the Eucharist in Catholicism is believed to be the actual body and blood of Jesus whereas it is consumed symbolically in Protestant religions **[15 marks]**

11.
- Agape is the highest form of love and charity and is the way that Christians should treat all human beings
- Additionally, it is recommended to discuss grace, which is God's unconditional love and mercy, given without humans having done anything to deserve it
- You may want to structure your answer into three categories for the body paragraphs: love of God to humans, the love that Christian practitioners show to God, and the love that Christian practitioners show to other humans.
- Connect agape to the love that Jesus showed to the most vulnerable people and to his teachings in the Gospels (books of Matthew, Mark, Luke, and John in the New Testament of the Christian Bible) **[15 marks]**

12.
- The Muslim community or umma, is united by following the Five Pillars of Islam
- The pillar of salat (prayer) is central to the lives of Muslims
- The ritual prayers are to be performed five times each day
- To properly perform the prayers, Muslims face towards Mecca
- Facing toward the same sacred city of Mecca at the same times unites Muslims around the world
- Muslims may pray at home, in a private space, or together in congregational prayers (jumu'ah), at mosques (places of worship in Islam) **[15 marks]**

13.
- The Qur'an receives its authority in Islam by being the word of Allah revealed to the prophet Muhammad (PBUH) through the angel Gabriel, according to Muslims
- The Qur'an is a concise text that focuses on the nature of Allah, the relationship between humans and Allah, and relationships among humans, as well as focusing on the significance of Allah's creations
- The Qur'an provides Muslims with rules to follow and determines what is allowed (halal) and what is forbidden (haram)
- The Hadith is the other major source in Islam and it is comprised of the Sunna (the teachings of the prophet Muhammad (PBUH)) and provides context for the Qur'an
- Sunni and Shia Muslims agree on its significance and the necessity of studying the Hadith in order to understand the meaning of the Qur'an and to understand Islam
- There are many verses in the Qur'an that command Muslims to live according to the life of the prophet Muhammad (PBUH), and without the Hadith practitioners would not be able to follow this command
- Both the Qur'an and the Hadith are considered primary sources and each provides practitioners with guidance and laws **[15 marks]**

14. Judaism:
- God is loving, all-knowing, and a creator
- God is generous because He created the universe and made humans in God's image
- God is forgiving as He forgave Adam and Eve for their sin in the Garden of Eden
- God is mysterious and cannot be understood in human form
- God, or G-d, or Yahweh ('I am what I am') is unnameable, because God is more powerful than humans and cannot be fully understood or named by them

Christianity:
- God is loving, all-knowing, and a creator
- God is generous because He created the universe and made humans in God's image
- God is forgiving as He forgave Adam and Eve for their sin in the Garden of Eden
- Through God's grace He sent mankind His son, Jesus
- God is united in the Trinity: God the Father, God the Son, and God the Holy Spirit

Islam:
- God is loving, all-knowing, and a creator
- God is generous because He created the universe and made humans in God's image
- God is beyond what humans can comprehend and cannot be rendered in human form
- The essence of being a Muslim is to submit to God or Allah
- The oneness of God (tawhid) is essential to His nature in Islam **[15 marks]**

Set B

Paper 1: Section A

1. (a) • The role of the self, or atman, in Hinduism
   • The role of karma as it relates to virtuous action and evil action and what the self 'becomes'
   • The role of dharma in connection to 'deeds' **[3 marks]**

(b) • Hindu practitioners' ultimate end goal is to achieve moksha
   • They can achieve moksha by focusing on various aspects of karma, samsara, and moksha throughout their lives
   • In order to liberate one's self from samsara, or the continuous cycle of birth and rebirth, an individual must acquire positive karma and uphold their given dharma
   • A Hindu practitioner can uphold their dharma and attain good karma by performing worship acts of puja
   • A Hindu practitioner can uphold their dharma and attain good karma by performing actions in accordance with their ashram, or stage in life.
   • If a Hindu practitioner acquires negative karma, or fails to uphold their dharma, they will not progress and elevate their next life status within the cycle of samsara
   • Negative karma prevents practitioners from attaining moksha, or liberation from the continuous cycle of samsara, which thus takes increased lifetimes **[6 marks]**

2. (a) • The Four Noble Truths as the main doctrine in which Siddhartha explained the root causes of human suffering
   • The root causes of suffering in Buddhism as Siddhartha laid out, which is unhealthy attachment
   • How 'cessation' is representative of nirvana, or the release from samsara **[3 marks]**

(b) • Buddhist practitioners believe in the Dhamma, or the word and doctrine of the original Buddha, Siddhartha Gautama
   • The Four Noble Truths is an element of the Dhamma in which Siddhartha described the universal truth of life
   • Consider describing the Four Noble Truths in depth, that life is suffering, which is caused by attachment and desire, but there is a way to relieve that suffering, which is through the Eightfold Path
   • Once a Buddhist practitioner can recognize the unhealthy attachments and desires in their lives, they can work to alleviate these desires through following the steps of the Eightfold Path
   • The Eightfold Path allows a practitioner to live according to the Middle Way, or lifestyle that emphasizes striking a balance between material items and aesthetic items **[6 marks]**

3. (a) • Sikhism emphasizes nam japna ('the repetition of God's name') in order to feel the presence of God
   • 'Thus were men saved in every direction' references the lesson of Guru Nanak that all people can access God directly without any formal rituals or involvement from priests
   • Through 'love and devotion' humans can feel God's presence because there is divinity in each person. Although there is divinity in each person, it is important to note that Sikhism is strictly monotheistic **[3 marks]**

(b) • The nature of God in Sikhism is all-knowing, timeless, formless and transcendent (beyond what humans can understand)
   • Sikhism is monotheistic, and although humans have jot (divine light within), God does not take human form
   • Sikh practitioners believe that God is sargun (personal and a driving force in the universe), as well as nirgun (infinite in qualities and forms)
   • God is often referred to as the Eternal One, or called Waheguru, to emphasize God's timelessness as the creator
   • People may strive to have gurmukh (a God-centered way of life that is in accordance with the Gurus) in order to achieve a union with God
   • The nature of God is revealed in Sikhism by the belief that God gave all people the ability to determine right from wrong, and therefore anyone can have a relationship with God **[6 marks]**

Paper 1: Section B

4. (a) • The nature of Judaism is monotheistic
   • God keeps promises with Jewish practitioners
   • According to Jewish practitioners, they are the chosen people of God **[3 marks]**

(b) • Abrahamic Covenant (God promised Abraham many descendants and a land of their own in exchange for devotion to God)
   • Mosaic Covenant (Moses received the Torah on Mt. Sinai and was told obedience to God would deliver Jewish practitioners out of slavery in Egypt)
   • Jewish practitioners are expected to adhere to the teachings of the Torah
   • The relationship between God and Jewish practitioners is compassionate and He protects His people
   • God expects that humans will show love and compassion to one another just as He has shown them
   • There is an unknowable nature of God in Judaism and He is transcendent (beyond what humans can comprehend) **[6 marks]**

5. (a) • God gives guidance to Christian practitioners and shows them what they should do to demonstrate their love for God.
   • God grants practitioners salvation (being saved from sin and its consequences)
   • Christian practitioners may enter the Kingdom of Heaven (the afterlife for Christian practitioners who led good lives) **[3 marks]**

(b) • Christian practitioners can show their devotion to God through the sacraments (Christian rituals)
   • Christian practitioners are saved from original sin (the sin first committed by Adam in the Christian Bible) by being baptized (cleansed of original sin)
   • God gave Christian practitioners free will and they can choose to live a life of doing good deeds and loving God
   • When practitioners sin, they can confess their sins and atone for (work to repair) their wrongdoings
   • Christian practitioners believe in the Trinity (God the Father, God the Son, and God the Holy Spirit)
   • In addition to believing in and loving God, Christian practitioners should practice agape (the highest form of love and charity) towards other people
   • God's grace (unconditional love and mercy from God, without humans having done anything to deserve it) delivers those who love God out of a life of sin **[6 marks]**

6. (a) • Allah is the creator of the universe
   • Muslims believe in the concept of tawhid which is the oneness and uniqueness of Allah
   • Muslims should praise Allah always by submitting to His will **[3 marks]**

(b) • Allah created all through His omnipotence (all-knowingness)
   • Therefore, Muslims should submit to Allah by believing in Him and praising Him
   • Muslims should struggle (jihad) to abide by the will of Allah as revealed to the prophet Muhammad (PBUH) through the Qur'an
   • Muslims should follow the teachings of the prophet Muhammad (PBUH) in the Hadith (the collection of teachings from the prophet Muhammad (PBUH))
   • Muslim practitioners believe in angels and prophets (messengers of Allah)
   • Practitioners adhere to the Five Pillars of Islam: profession of faith, prayer, almsgiving, fasting, and pilgrimage in order to demonstrate their daily devotion to Allah **[6 marks]**

Paper 1: Section C

7. (a) • Define the Tao as the absolute principal underlying everything in the universe
   • Describe the Tao as neither being described or conceived in thought by humans
   • The goal of humans is to subscribe to wu wei and live in accordance with the Tao and 'the essence of all life' **[3 marks]**

(b) • A Taoist practitioner can connect with The Profound Mystery by striking a harmonious balance through subscribing to the principals of Yin Yang
   • Balance and harmony are achieved by practicing Wu Wei, doing nothing that is unnatural, strained, or artificial
   • Practical applications can be made through practicing the art of tai chi
   • A Taoist practitioner can connect with the profound mystery by employing the Three Vehicles: good deeds, ritual and ceremonies, and the art of transformation of the mind

- Tai chi, meditation, and other mechanisms help a practitioner maintain balance and harness the Chi, or the life force which runs throughout every individual
- Taoist practitioners can also cultivate the Eight Virtues which teach one how to live harmoniously and balance relationships with others and with the community **[6 marks]**

8. **(a)**
- Jain practitioners should practice ahimsa, which is non-violence towards any living being
- Ahimsa is the most important aspect of the Five Great Vows and the single most important aspect of Jainism
- Jain practitioners experience the happiness and suffering of others and should engage in suffering to lighten the karma of the soul (jiva) **[3 marks]**

(b)
- Ahimsa, or non-violence, is central to the teachings of Jainism
- Jain practitioners should have right knowledge, right faith, and right conduct to achieve the goal of liberation
- To harm another creature is to harm oneself because all creatures are connected through karma, which determines how one will be reborn
- Jain practitioners are impacted by others' suffering and cannot be indifferent to it
- Right thoughts, actions and deeds regarding ahimsa mean that speaking harshly to someone or thinking evil thoughts about someone are forbidden in addition to physical non-violence
- All actions, thoughts, words and deeds have an effect (karma) and karma sticks to the soul (jiva) **[6 marks]**

9. **(a)**
- The 'body of humankind' refers to the Bahá'í belief that all humans are unified in a worldwide community
- 'Be a lamp to those...' suggests that Bahá'í practitioners should learn the teachings of Bahá'u'lláh
- 'Guiding light to the feet of the erring' encourages Bahá'í practitioners to develop divine aspects of themselves to live in accordance with God's plan for the world

(b)
- Bahá'í practitioners believe in the unity and equality of all people as being from a single race, therefore it is important to treat all people with respect **[3 marks]**
- Bahá'í practitioners believe in the validity of other religions and that the differences are due to differences in culture
- Bahá'í practitioners believe that no group of people should consider itself to be superior to another and should regard any disadvantages suffered by a group as immoral
- All people can develop divine aspects of themselves to live in accordance with God's plan for the world
- Bahá'í practitioners believe in the importance of charity to reduce the amount of poverty worldwide
- The Bahá'í faith advocates for human rights and believes in a world of human rights **[6 marks]**

SET B

Paper 2: Section A

1.
- In order to acquire good karma, or generate a positive force to elevate one's standing in the next stage of samsara (rebirth, one must complete their dharma
- Dharma, simply put, is the duty a practitioner has to their life in this current stage of the samsara cycle. There are multiple ways to complete one's duty, including partaking in yoga to become closer to God and participating in various puja (rituals) to worship God
- Another way to complete one's duty (or dharma) is to carry out one's responsibility according to one's varna (more popularly known as caste)
- A varna is a social classification of a person based on their personality and inclination for work. There are four varnas in the caste system in many Hindu societies today
- The four traditional varnas are the:
  – Brahmins – priests, scholars, and teachers
  – Kshatriyas – warriors and administrators
  – Vaishyas – farmers and merchants
  – Shudras – labourers or those in the service industry
- Contrary to popular belief, the varna classification is not inherently rigid, and should allow for social mobility. The classifications are meant to allow for an orderly society designed to complement one's personality and affinity for the type of work chosen

- Whichever type of work a person chooses to pursue, they must do it with love and devotion to God and to society in order to fulfil their dharmic duty. **[15 marks]**

2.
- Identify that there are multiple yogic paths that a practitioner can choose to practice, depending on which path is the right one for them
- What is the most 'appropriate' path lies in the eye of the Hindu practitioner, because Hinduism is a pluralistic religion, meaning that there are multiple paths to achieve the end goal which is moksha, liberation from the cycle of samsara (the continuous cycle of birth and rebirth)
- Yoga is referenced in many of Hinduism's sacred texts, particularly within the Vedas and the Bhagavad Gita. The Vedas give a very specific and direct description, while The Bhagavad Gita is an allegorical dialogue between an avatar (or human incarnation) of Brahman in Krishna, and Arjuna, a royal individual navigating a battlefield, which represents the battles of life. The allegorical dialogue has Krishna coaching Arjuna in how to achieve union with Brahman
- The four main paths a practitioner can choose from are karma, Raja, Gyana, and Bhatki
- Bhatki is the path of love, karma is the act of good intention and deeds, Raja is that of psychophysical exercises, and Gyana is a philosophical path through intellectual pursuits of study
- These paths are separate, but also interdependent, as one cannot embark on only one path without considering elements of the other paths
- A person who deems Raja yoga to be appropriate for them will embark on disciplined psychophysical exercises that involve focused breathing and asanas, or movements. Breathing techniques include pranayama breathing
- Through breathing, a Hindu practitioner will attempt to connect to the Supreme God force, Brahma, through deliberate exercises and through recitation of the sacred syllable 'om'
- Raja yoga involves a continual and deliberate experimentation of physical exercises
- These movements allow a person to connect both body and mind, and work toward uncovering their inner atman, the soul or inner Brahman. This allows a person to discern between the 'false' self, or the self that is motivated and ruled by the material world, and the 'higher' self that is internal and connected to Brahman **[15 marks]**

3.
- Most Buddhist practitioners share the same core beliefs in the Three Jewels, that is the Buddha, the Dhamma and the Sangha
- Regarding the Buddha and the Dhamma (the role of Siddhartha and his word, or the doctrine of Buddhism), most Buddhist practitioners also follow core pieces of doctrine such as the Four Noble Truths and the Eightfold Path
- Buddhist practitioners of different sects, such as Theravada and Mahayana sects, will interpret different portions of Siddhartha's life to inform their beliefs in worship, attainment of enlightenment and personal values
- Mahayana means 'big raft'. Buddhist practitioners believe in a 'big raft' philosophy, meaning the goal for Buddhists should be to seek enlightenment and nirvana, but to also help others across too
- Mahayana practitioners will interpret the point of Siddhartha's life when he adopted aesthetic principles as being when he was on the brink of starvation while meditating and seeking enlightenment. In an act of grace and compassion, a woman approaches him with a bowl of rice. He later attributes the woman's action as aiding him on the path toward enlightenment
- Mahayana Buddhists will interpret this act as critical and representative of their values and actions. Therefore, Mahayana Buddhists value compassion as their core principal which aids practitioners toward enlightenment
- Theravada Buddhists, on the other hand, value wisdom as a core principal which shall set someone on the path to enlightenment. They believe that the meditative moments when Siddhartha is reaching the truth and enlightenment beneath the Bodhi Tree are the ones in which Siddhartha can understand The Four Noble Truths
- Therefore, individuality and wisdom are the core principles emphasized in Theravada Buddhism **[15 marks]**

4.
- The idea that tanha (craving) and dukkha (suffering) are interconnected is a major belief in Buddhism, as cravings and desires drive one's suffering

- It is imperative that a Buddhist practitioner recognizes portions of the Four Noble Truths and applies them to their own lives: that life is suffering (dukkha), suffering is caused by desires and cravings (tanha), that there is a way to overcome these sufferings, and that the way is through the Eightfold Path
- Since tanha and dukkha are clearly outlined in the first and second Four Noble Truths, their interconnection is undeniable
- In the life of a Buddhist practitioner, if one is overly attached to cravings and desires, then they have the ability to overtake one's mental and emotional states
- Over attachment causes a practitioner to focus on the attachment and therefore suffering, and prevents them from maintaining a compassionate disposition in the world and overcoming suffering to attain enlightenment and nirvana
- The Eightfold Path, or Middle Way, is the Fourth Noble Truth. This outlines the various steps which one must employ to conquer tanha and therefore alleviate dukkha, such as right speech and right action
- A Buddhist practitioner who lives life in recognition that life is suffering, but that there is a way to overcome suffering through working toward the steps of the Eightfold Path, recognizes that it is imperative to overcome cravings to mitigate suffering and therefore achieve enlightenment **[15 marks]**

5.
- Sikh practitioners believe in the cycle of birth and rebirth, and also that karma will affect one's position in the next life. One's karma consists of both positive and negative deeds that one has done that affect the determining of this position in the next life
- God, according to Sikhism, consists of one all-knowing entity that is genderless and without form. There is only one supreme being
- While Sikh practitioners exert great free will in their karmic actions and influence over the process of their rebirth, it is ultimately God's grace which aids in their salvation (mukti) and escape from the cycle of rebirth
- Mukti comes, then, as a result of God's grace, and not solely as something humans have earned
- In Sikh doctrine and through the teachings of various gurus, a Sikh practitioner is expected to learn the ways in which it is possible to become close to God, and eventually achieve mukti
- Sikh practitioners must recognize the presence of God in themselves and within others, but do so authentically and truthfully, as pretending to exhibit such feelings inauthentically will not mean true devotion and recognition of God for an individual
- Pragmatically, three duties can be carried out at all times which allow a Sikh practitioner to know God and achieve eventual mukti, called 'the Three Deeds': Pray, Work, and Give
- A Sikh practitioner must pray while keeping God in mind at all times, work honestly and earn an honest living, and live a life of charity and giving to others
- Avoiding self-destructive behaviours which take away from one's ability to know God prolong mukti or salvation. Living life as a member of God's community, recognizing God within themselves and others, and conducting one's life honestly and in completing charitable deeds all help a practitioner to understand God **[15 marks]**

6.
- Sikhism emphasizes the oneness of God that is incomprehensible, formless, and timeless. Many Sikh gurus shaped religious beliefs around this concept
- Two gurus who shaped Sikhism and its beliefs were the first of the gurus, Guru Nanak, and the last of the gurus, Guru Gobind Singh
- Guru Nanak was responsible for many of the foundational beliefs that form the basis of Sikhism
- Guru Nanak lived in the 15th century and achieved enlightenment after meditation on a river bank for over three days. Afterward, he reported to having experienced a powerful vision regarding the divine, the human experience and the nature of life. He recorded this into a song entitled 'Japji Sahib' or 'Song of the Soul'
- Japji Sahib became the foundation for Guru Nanak's teachings. He spent the rest of his life teaching about the oneness of God, brotherhood and sisterhood of all across all religions and socioeconomic backgrounds, and the internal divinity within all of humanity
- The last of the Sikh Gurus, Guru Gobind Singh, established the Khalsa Order (or the pure soldier-saints of Sikhism), honoured for their reverence to the Sikh Code of Conduct, including proper dress and hairstyle (uncut), with a turban for men

- Guru Gobind Singh removed priests from the Sikh order, feeling that they had suffered from corruption and that Sikh practitioners needed only to rely on the sacred text of Sri Guru Granth Sahib (or the 'Eternal Guru of the Sikhs'). This scripture contains the poetry of all the Gurus, along with writings of saints of other faiths whose thoughts were consistent with those of the Sikh Gurus **[15 marks]**

7. **Hinduism:**
- Brahman exists in a limitless form, hence the reference of 'Brahman the Limitless'
- The limitless forms are communicated to humans through murti, or means of communication with Brahman, which usually manifest in lesser deity forms such as the trimurti, consisting of Brahma, Shiva, and Vishnu, or through avatars, human incarnations such as Krishna in The Bhagavad Gita
- Monism refers to a theory in which everything in existence can be reduced to one entity, and in Hinduism, that is Brahman. This means the most minute entity to the most enormous are all equal in existence, as Brahman exists within them
- Brahman exists as an omnipresent, eternal, and spiritual source of the universe
- Brahman also exists as the universal truth that all beings will come to know upon reaching moksha, or spiritual liberation from samsara (the cycle of birth and rebirth for all life)
- The atman is the inner self, or soul, and is a part of Brahman that practitioners seek to uncover through aesthetic practice and through yoga, thereby reaching union with Brahman

Buddhism:
- Worshipping a God might occur depending on the Buddhist sect; however, Buddhism generally refuses to confirm or deny the existence of a God. While Siddhartha Gautama is the revered and holy founder of Buddhism, he is not considered God in Buddhism
- Siddhartha Gautama, however, had divine qualities unlike those who came before him, which allowed him to reach the truth in enlightenment, or spiritual awakening to the truth, while sitting beneath the Bodhi Tree in Northern India
- The doctrine of Buddhism is related to the word, or Dhamma, of Siddhartha. This consists of core sacred texts such as the Four Noble Truths and the Eightfold Path. The Dhamma, along with the Sangha, or Buddhist community, and the Buddha, make up the cornerstone of Buddhist worship, and cannot exist one without the others. For example, the Dhamma is powerless without the Sangha to support and translate, and the power of the Sangha is rooted in the Dhamma
- In Theravada and Mahayana Buddhism, there are holy figures who have lived their lives in accordance to the Buddha and are revered as individuals with divine qualities. In Mahayana Buddhism, this individual is referred to as a bodhisattva, and in Theravada Buddhism this individual is referred to as an arhat
- Both sects interpret differing parts of the Buddha's life to inform their beliefs and practice

Sikhism:
- Sikhism is a monotheistic religion that emphasizes some of the same religious beliefs as Hinduism and Buddhism, but the role of God is intercession in a practitioner's salvation (mukti)
- To Sikh practitioners, God can neither be envisioned nor fully understood, but is all-knowing and the only supreme being
- Sikhs interpret God as rewarding them for their positive deeds and actions as they move through the cycle of samsara (birth and rebirth), with grace and ultimate salvation. Therefore, God is interpreted as one whose ultimate authority determines the practitioner's next life or mukti, but based on what that practitioner has done in this life
- It is the responsibility of a Sikh practitioner to become one with God, and work to engender their relationship authentically. In this way, they interpret God as a force that they can cultivate a relationship with throughout their lives **[15 marks]**

Paper 2: Section B

8.
- Humans are born with yetzer hara (evil inclination)
- Life for Jewish practitioners is a struggle between yetzer hara (evil inclination) and yetzer ha-tov (good inclination)
- Humans were given free will by God and can choose to do good

- Guidance on how to live a good life is central to the Torah
- The Torah includes 613 mitvot (commandments) that detail how to be a good Jewish practitioner and live a life of yetzer ha-tov (good inclination) and can be broken down into several categories
- The decalogue are the first 10 commandments of the 613 mitvot and are perhaps considered the most important as they give guidance on how to live in a way that is good to oneself and good to others
- However, there are other detailed kashrut (dietary) laws in the Torah regarding keeping kosher that arguably do not relate to the quote above **[15 marks]**

9.
- Tikkun olam means to repair or improve the world
- The world was created by God and is innately good; however, because God gave humans free will, humans have committed sins and those sins have had a negative impact on the world
  - Actions of treating people better, often considered mitzvoth (or religious duties) are intended to help those who are vulnerable and to make the world more harmonious
- It is important to note that the term tikkun olam does not appear in the Torah, but it does appear in the Mishnah, the rabbinical teachings that make up the first part of the Talmud
- Tikkun olam means that Jewish practitioners should take responsibility for the well-being of society and in the present day many Jewish practitioners consider it to be social justice
- Some Jewish practitioners may connect the need to repair the world back to the exile of the Jewish people, while others may even trace the need to repair the world back to the exile of Adam and Eve from the Garden of Eden in the book of Genesis.
- Some have argued that the Jewish diaspora (the dispersal of Jewish individuals across many different lands) gives Jewish practitioners a consciousness of exile and an awareness of the need to repair the world. **[15 marks]**

10.
- Actual sin relates to evil acts that go against the will of God. In contrast, original sin relates to the sinful acts and tendencies that are part of us from birth. Original sin manifests itself in actual sins.
- Genesis, the first book of the Christian Bible, is the the source for the teachings about original sin
- The implications of original sin for humans
- Baptism is a way to be cleansed of original sin
- Free will and the understanding that sometimes humans sin
- Ways to be free from sin include confession (one of the sacraments to formally confess one's sins), redemption (being saved from sin), reconciliation (the act of healing one's relationship with God), repentance (sincere remorse for wrongdoings) and atonement (reparation of sins)
- God's grace (unconditional love and mercy from God, without humans having done anything to deserve it) and Christian practitioners' ability to show agape (highest form of Christian love and charity) despite being marked with original sin
- Conclude: by considering how God's loving nature in Christianity has impacted the ability of Christian practitioners to overcome original sin **[15 marks]**

11.
- The goal in Christianity is to achieve salvation (being saved from sin and its consequences)
- The ultimate reward is to enter the Kingdom of Heaven (the Christian afterlife which is free from sin)
- Christian practitioners believe in the Trinity (God the Father, God the Son, and God the Holy Spirit)
- Christian practitioners also believe that Jesus is their Saviour
- Christian practitioners should live a life of loving God and doing good deeds as outlined by the laws in the Old Testament of the Christian Bible and the teachings of Jesus in the New Testament of the Christian Bible
- In addition to believing in and loving God, Christian practitioners should practice agape (the highest form of love and charity) towards other people
- God's grace (unconditional love and mercy from God, without humans having done anything to deserve it) delivers those who love God out of a life of sin
- The goal of salvation impacts the entire life of a Christian practitioner to live according to Jesus's teachings **[15 marks]**

12.
- Women hold an elevated status in Islam and that women and men are considered equals in that they are both expected to follow the Five Pillars of Islam

- Islam improved the role and status of women when the religion was established in the 7th century as compared with other societies at that time
- Khadijah, the prophet Muhammad's (PBUH) first wife and the first follower of the prophet was important because she believed Him and supported Him when He had His revelations
- The status of Khadijah as a successful businesswoman and an older widow at the time she married the prophet Muhammad (PBUH)
- There are different modern day discussions about the hijab (the headscarf worn by Muslim women)
- Reasons women choose to wear the hijab in free countries is to show an outward sign of their profession of faith in Allah and to demonstrate modesty
- Modesty is important for both men and women to guard and protect in Islam and is referenced in the Qur'an
- The term hijab in Arabic means 'barrier' or 'partition' and has a range of interpretations **[15 marks]**

13.
- Allah is loving, all-knowing, and a creator
- Allah is generous because He created the universe and made humans in God's image
- Allah is beyond what humans can comprehend and cannot be rendered in human form
- The essence of being a Muslim is to submit to Allah
- To profess one's faith in Allah is the first pillar of the Five Pillars of Islam (shahadah)
- The oneness of God (tawhid) is essential to His nature in Islam
- The concept of tawhid is key to the understanding of monotheism in Islam **[15 marks]**

14. Judaism:
- Eschatology is the beliefs in the afterlife or what happens after death for an individual and for all humans
- Jewish practitioners believe that the world to come is important, but the emphasis is on this world and repairing it (tikkun olam)
- While there are teachings about the Messianic Age and the belief that the Messiah will come at that time
- There is disagreement on this concept between Orthodox and Reform Jewish practitioners
- Orthodox Movement that believes a messiah sent by God will usher in the Messianic Age
- There are no clear descriptions of the afterlife in the Torah
- Many Jewish practitioners in the Reform Movement focus on the ethical implications of Judaism and seek to do good deeds to repair the world rather than focusing on the Messianic Age

Christianity:
- Christian practitioners believe in the afterlife as being the Kingdom of Heaven
- The Christian bible describes heaven in various verses throughout the New Testament as a place of no death or mourning
- The book of Revelation discusses the apocalypse, the end of days, and the second coming of Jesus
- Humans will be judged to determine whether they go to the Kingdom Heaven or to Hell
- Christian practitioners can reach the Kingdom of Heaven by believing in God, participating in the sacraments to show their devotion to God, and living a life of good deeds according to the teachings of Jesus

Islam:
- Muslims believe in akhirah (afterlife)
- Muslims believe in the Day of Judgement on which all people will be tried in accordance with their actions
- Muslims will either go to Janna, an afterlife often described as a garden paradise without pain or sorrow
- Or they are sent to Jahannam (hellfire) which is a place of torment and misery
- Muslims can reach Janna by believing in Allah, adhering to the Five Pillars, and living a life of good deeds according to the teachings of the prophet Muhammad (PBUH)
- Janna and Jahannam are described in detail in the Qur'an and these descriptions can serve as reminders to practitioners that this world is temporary **[15 marks]**

Set C

> The Set C answers are written out in full so, along with testing your knowledge on the subject itself, you can see how you could structure your answer and link your points together in proper sentences and paragraphs.

Paper 1: Section A

1. (a) The first teaching in this passage is that all beings are one and the same. The atman or individual soul is also Brahman or the universal soul, 'He who sees everything in his atman and his atman in everything.' The second teaching in this passage is that once there is a realization of this oneness, that atman and Brahman are one and the same, there will be no more perplexity and sorrow ends. The third teaching is that the atman, or the self, is bodiless, transcendent and pervades all. **[3 marks]**

(b) In Hinduism there is a belief that the individual soul in all living beings, the atman, is in ignorance (maya) of the true nature of reality. As long as the atman is in ignorance of its true self and the nature of reality, it is caught in a cycle of reincarnation or samsara. In samsara the soul is continuously reborn into a new body. The most important goal of a Hindu's religious life is release from this tiring cycle of perpetual rebirth through moksha, or liberation from samsara. When the soul achieves moksha, it is released from the process of samsara and becomes one with the universal Brahman. A Hindu practitioner must work towards liberation, thus human effort is an important aspect of liberation. An atman's rebirth is dependent on karma, or action. Positive action may lead to a positive reincarnation or moksha. Brahman refers to the universal consciousness or God. Brahman is the cause of all that exists. The highest kind of knowledge is Jnana yoga, which is defined as direct knowledge of the ultimate reality, or realization of the oneness of the universe. When there is a realization that atman and Brahman are one and the same, liberation is possible. This is called monism or Advaita Vedanta, developed by Adi Shankara in the 8th century. There are other views regarding atman and Brahman: another school of Vedanta, Dvaita, argues that atman and Brahman are separate entities, and that the atman can achieve moksha through worship of Vishnu. **[6 marks]**

2. (a) The first teaching in this passage is that 'people followed by thirst crawl around like a captured hare' this refers to the Buddhist belief that suffering is the result of craving or thirst (tanha). People who have cravings are eventually dissatisfied or experience Dukkha, or suffering. The second teaching is that people who are consumed by craving are 'captured' in samsara: they are born and then reborn again and again in a cycle of samsara or reincarnation. The third teaching in this passage is that Buddhists should strive to remove this thirst or control their desires. **[3 marks]**

(b) Tanha is a Pali word that means thirst, desire or greed but it is usually translated as craving. It is a central concept in Buddhism and is mentioned in the Four Noble Truths. The First Noble Truth states that life is suffering or Dukkha and so all human beings experience this suffering or unsatisfactoriness. According to the Second Noble Truth, tanha is the cause of dukkha and the cycle of perpetual rebirths (samsara). There are different kinds of cravings. Buddhism outlines three main kinds of craving, the craving for physical and sensual pleasure, such as craving fine food or sexual pleasure; the craving of existence or being, which is described as the craving to be something, or have important status in this world, but is also the desire for improved status in rebirth; and finally the craving for nonexistence, or not wanting to experience unpleasant experiences (suicide is an example of this type of craving). According to the principle of dependent origination, or Pratītyasamutpāda, tanha is seen as one of the reasons why we are born as humans and it keeps us trapped in a cycle of repeated rebirths. Suffering and rebirth will not end until craving is eradicated. Practitioners must detach from their cravings if they are to achieve the goal of Buddhism, which is nirvana. Nirvana cannot be achieved if we still have craving. The Third Noble Truth explains that suffering (Dukkha) can end if we end craving and eliminate the fires of craving, greed and desire. To do this this, practitioners should follow the Eightfold path, or the Middle Way, as outlined by the Buddha. **[6 marks]**

3. (a) The first teaching in this passage is that there is One Creator or one God, in Sikhism, commonly referred to as Ik onkar. The second teaching in this passage concerns the central characteristics of God according to Sikhism, that the One Creator is the creator of all things, is also timeless, and is an eternal truth. The third teaching in this passage is that the grace or favour of a teacher is needed to make people aware of this One Creator, commenting on the importance of the guru in realizing God. **[3 marks]**

(b) The term guru can have various meanings. The central scared Text in Sikhism is the Guru Granth Sahib and it opens with the above verse, known as the Mul Mantar. This forms the Sikh creed; it contains central beliefs about the nature of the 'One Creator', and the realization of this eternal truth. In Sikhism the guru is central to a Sikh's experience of this eternal truth. The last line of the Mul Mantar states that the guidance or grace of a guru or teacher is necessary to make the One creator known to human beings. In one sense, the guru is the sacred text or Shabad, the word, found in the Guru Granth Sahib and other Sikh sacred texts, that makes God known to human beings. However, the guru in Sikhism also refers to the founder of the religion, Guru Nanak, or any one of the 10-human guru's in Sikh history. The last of these human gurus, Guru Gobind Singh, collected Sikh sacred writing in the Guru Granth Sahib, and declared it the Eternal Guru of the Sikhs. The Guru Granth Sahib replaced the human gurus. The guru or teacher can also be understood to be the One Creator or God. A long tradition of Guru-Chela, or guru disciple relationships, has also developed in Sikhism. **[6 marks]**

Paper 1: Section B

4. (a) This is the Shema, a very important prayer in Judaism. The first teaching contained in this passage is monotheism, or the belief in one God. The prayer declares, 'Hear, O Israel, the Lord is our God, the Lord is one.' The second teaching in this passage is that Jews are commanded to love the Lord with all their heart, soul and might. Jews must focus all their energy on loving God. By loving God Jews are following their good inclination or yetzer ha-tov. The third teaching in this passage is that keeping the Shema in one's heart is a commandment, 'Keep these words that I am commanding you today in your heart'. **[3 marks]**

(b) The Shema reminds the Jews that they are the chosen people, chosen to be an example to all humans of worship and obedience to God. Traditional or observant Jews view the recitation of the Shema twice a day, in the morning and evening, as a biblical commandment. The Shema reminds Jews that they need to focus on God in all aspects of their lives, and follow their good inclination (yetzer ha-tov). Jews are expected to live according to the Shema. This means they should keep the commandments (Mitzvot) and instructions in the Shema alive by teaching them to their children. The Shema goes on to say Jews should remind themselves of the importance of the Shema by binding the prayer 'as a sign on your hand and let them serve as a symbol on your forehead, inscribe them on the doorposts of your house and on your gates.' The tefillin contains the Shema prayer handwritten on paper and placed in cubic black leather boxes with leather straps that are bound on the arms and forehead during prayer. Orthodox Jewish men live according to the Shema by wearing the Shema in tefillin. Observant Jews also place a mezuzah on their doorstops, to remind themselves to live according to the Shema's instructions. Mezuzahs are decorative boxes, containing a piece of parchment with the handwritten Shema prayer. They are placed on the doorstop of observant Jewish homes. **[6 marks]**

5. (a) The first teaching in this passage is that the blood of Jesus purifies us of all sin and redeems us. This is a reference to Jesus dying for our sins. The second teaching in this passage is the universality of sin: we all sin and should acknowledge this truth. The third teaching in this passage is that if practitioners confess their sins and repent, God will forgive and purify them. God is described as faithful and just, forgiving those sins and delivering practitioners from sin. **[3 marks]**

(b) Sin is a central doctrine in Christianity. The message of Christianity is that practitioners have the opportunity to find redemption in Jesus Christ. The bible tells us that God created human beings in his own image. This is usually understood to mean that human beings have the ability to use reason to understand the world and their relationship to God (unlike, for example, animals). The purpose of life in Christianity is to love and serve God, in return for God's grace. When humans go against God's will this is called sin. According to chapters 2–3 of the Bible, God first created Adam and Eve and placed them in the Garden of Eden. He forbade them to eat the fruit of the tree of knowledge of good and evil. Tempted by Satan, they defied his rule and ate the apple. God then banished them from the Garden of Eden, and condemned humanity to hard work, disease and death. Christians refer to this incident as the fall. The fall is the result of a lapse of reason. Sin is a rejection of or separation from God. This story helps us understand the Christian view of sin as universal and inevitable. Every human being is equally capable of sin. Human beings frequently go against God's will and choose to follow their own selfish desires and ignore God's plan and design. There is a diversity of belief regarding sin in different Christian denominations. Some Christians believe in the doctrine of original sin, which argues that the original sin of Adam and Eve is passed on to all following generations, while others argue that sin originates with Satan, who tempts people away from God's will. However, despite mankind's potential for sin, this does not mean that God does not love and forgive us. Redemption is possible for all. **[6 marks]**

6. (a) The first teaching in this passage is that death is certain: all souls will die and be judged for their thoughts and deeds on Judgement Day. The verse reminds Muslims that they cannot escape death. The second teaching is that Muslims will be judged for their beliefs and actions in this life. The third teaching is that those who attain heaven have achieved the real 'object of life'. The verse also comments on the nature of this life, or Hayat Al Dunia, which is described as 'but goods and chattels of deception'. The real goal of life is 'the Garden' or heaven, in Al Akhira or the afterlife. **[3 marks]**

   (b) Belief in an afterlife is a central tenet of Islam. It is one of the articles of faith in Sunni Islam. Muslims believe that this world (Al Dunia) is a preparation for the next life (Al Akhirah). Muslims believe in a day of judgement and the physical existence of heaven and hell. Physical death in Islam is not the end; in fact, this life is only the prelude for the more important spiritual life and the closeness to Allah that awaits practitioners in the afterlife. Belief in Judgement day and an afterlife are essential articles of faith in Islam. Muslims believe that everyone will stand before Allah on Judgement day and will be judged for their beliefs and actions. Muslims believe it is impossible to know who will go to heaven and who will go to hell, but faith in Allah and the truth of his revelations, as well as trying to live according to those revelations, will be rewarded. A Muslim seeking rewards in Heaven on Judgement day is expected to follow the Five Pillars of Islam. The Five Pillars outline the actions or religious duties of Muslims. Practitioners following the Five Pillars of Islam (the declaration of faith in Allah and his messenger the prophet Muhammad (PBUH)), praying five times a day, giving charity or Zakat, fasting during the holy month of Ramadan and finally making pilgrimage or hajj to Mecca (if possible), will be rewarded with heaven. Heaven is described in the Qur'an as a garden with rivers where the faithful will rest. On the other hand, hell is described as a terrible inferno where those who disobeyed Allah will be punished for their sins. There is evidence in the Qu'ran that non-Muslim can also attain paradise and even those who have acted badly still have a chance to attain paradise by Allah's grace. **[15 marks]**

Paper 1: Section C

7. (a) The first teaching in the passage is that the Dao does nothing. This is a reference to the Dao, or the 'way' or the natural law of the universe. The Dao is described in terms of opposites: it does nothing but leaves nothing undone. This is a reference to wu wei or the law of non-action, to do by not doing. The second teaching in this passage is that wu wei or non-action is the way to the Tao. If one becomes one with the Dao or understands the flow of this universal law, wu wei will be enabled. The third teaching in this passage is a reference to the applications of Daoism in politics. If political leaders were at one with the Dao, all creation would benefit. **[3 marks]**

   (b) The main message of Daoism is living in harmony with the Dao. The Dao is the 'way' but is a difficult concept to explain; Daoist practitioners themselves claim that the Dao is beyond language. The Dao is the natural order of the universe. Living in harmony with the Dao is wu wei. One of the central concepts of Daoism is the doctrine of wu wei, commonly translated as non-doing or doing nothing. However, it would be a misunderstanding to conclude that Daoism encourages doing nothing. One way to think of this doctrine is as the action of non-action. In other words, wu wei is the act of taking no action that is not in line or in flow with the natural order of the universe or the Dao. Wu wei is not going against the natural order of things or the natural flow and not attempting to force things to happen. Therefore, wu wei is acting naturally or acting in accordance with the natural world or Dao. Wu wei is effortless but achieving wu wei requires some effort. Many Daoist practitioners withdraw into meditation to achieve the Dao. Wu wei comes as a result of oneness with

the Dao. The ideal person or sage in Daoism is at one with the Dao and therefore acts effortlessly or has wu wei. Many Daoist practitioners believe that immortality is achievable as a result of oneness with the Dao, expressed through meditation and wu wei. In Daoism, practitioners are often encouraged to be like water, flexible and flowing. If practitioners, like water, submit to the laws of nature, they will achieve wu wei as a result of oneness with the Dao and will experience things effortlessly. **[6 marks]**

8. (a) The first teaching in this passage is about the nature of karma. Jains believe that karma is an actual substance. This substance sticks to us as a result of our actions. The second teaching in this passage is that karma occurs as a result of our thoughts. The third teaching is that the transformation of the molecules into karma is not caused by the jiva but rather is a natural law. **[3 marks]**

   (b) Jains believe that every living thing has a soul, or a jiva. As a result of their actions, souls accumulate karma. Jains see karma as a form of matter or very fine particles, and the accumulation of these karma particles draws the soul back into a body at the time of death, stopping it from achieving liberation. Karma is everything in Jainism. Jains believe the universe is eternal, has no beginning and no end, and runs according to cosmic laws that do not require a creator. However, it would be wrong to assume Jains do not believe in gods. They believe we each have the potential to become a God. In this sense, gods in Jainism are souls (jivas) who have been liberated from the constant cycle of rebirths. A jiva can only be liberated from rebirth if it eliminates all its karma. Karma in Jainism is attached to souls as a result of their ignorance. The aim of Jainism is to eliminate karma and thus achieve liberation. Jains uphold these principles by practicing vegetarianism and non-violence in thought, deed and action. In Jainism it is not only bad karma that leads to rebirth but also good karma. Jains divide up karma into eight main types, which is divided into four kinds: karma as a result of attachment to worldly things; karma accumulated as a result of emotions or passionate feelings, such as hate, love or greed; karma as a result of sensual or physical enjoyment; and finally karma accumulated as a result of ignorance. The first three types of karma can be addressed by eliminating attachments to worldly objects, strong emotions and sensual pleasures. Jain monks take the five vows to eliminate karma. They vow to do no harm and uphold non-violence (Ahimsa), to speak truth (Satya), to not steal (Asteya), to not commit adultery (Brahmacharya), and to limit one's possessions (Aparigraha). **[6 marks]**

9. (a) The first teaching in this passage is that the human soul is 'fashioned after the nature of God' and can manifest godlike qualities. The second teaching in this passage is that each human being is born with a pure and holy soul. The third teaching in this passage is that while human beings come into this world with a pure soul, as they go through life, they have the potential to acquire virtues (good qualities) or vices (bad qualities). **[3 marks]**

   (b) Bahá'i believe that we are born with a pure, holy and immortal soul. However, human beings are also born with a dual nature: a physical nature and a spiritual nature. The physical or 'lower nature' is associated with negative aspects of human behaviour. The second aspect is the spiritual or 'higher nature'. It is viewed as rational and able to come closer to God and reflect divine attributes. If human beings focus on their spiritual nature, they can reflect the attributes of God. This is the purpose of life according to Bahá'i, for each practitioner to realize their potential and to manifest as many of the divine's attributes as possible. These divine attributes include love, justice, patience and wisdom. Bahá'i do not believe in heaven and hell as a physical place. According to Bahá'i, the idea of heaven and hell should be understood symbolically as nearness or distance from God. Heaven is attaining the presence of God. In order to develop their spiritual nature human beings must detach from the physical world and focus on the spiritual. The attachments of the physical world stop the soul from progressing and coming closer to God. A Bahá'i practitioner can develop their spiritual nature through prayer, reading the Bahá'i scripture, loving God, and service to humanity. The purpose of this life is to gain spiritual virtues for the next life. **[6 marks]**

SET C

Paper 2: Section A

1. It cannot be denied that Ahimsa or non-violence is an important belief in Hinduism and other Indic religions. The term Ahimsa means

'Do no harm' in Sanskrit and it forms the foundation of Hindu ethical thought. Ahimsa is a physical state of refraining from violent action but also refers to a mental state free of anger or hate. Despite its central position in Hindu traditions and its importance in both Hindu belief and practice, it is important to note that Hinduism is not a wholly pacifist religion. Hindu sacred texts, such as the Bhagavad Gita, justify the use of violence by members of certain castes and under certain circumstances.

Ahimsa is inspired by central beliefs in Hinduism. It is related to the belief that an individual's soul is a manifestation of the divine universal soul or Brahman. An essential realization in Hinduism is that atman and Brahman are one, or that all individual souls are one and part of the ultimate or universal soul, Brahman. This realization is seen as essential for moksha or liberation from samsara, the cycle of death and rebirth. This belief that all living beings contain a spark of the divine promotes non-violent behaviour towards all living beings. Ahimsa is also connected to the concepts of karma and samsara in Hinduism. Karma means action: in Hinduism all action leads to karma but negative actions, such as harmful or violent actions, lead to negative karma and this negative karma will influence an individual's rebirth.

Hinduism encourages restraint and non-violence; however, it would be incorrect to assume that Hinduism forbids all violence. The Bhagavad Gita, one of the most revered of the Hindu sacred texts, contains a conversation between Arjuna and the god Krishna, in which Krishna clearly presents the argument that it is Arjuna's duty, as a member of the warrior Kshatriya caste, to fight in a just war. Despite Arjuna's reluctance to participate in the violent conflict, Krishna reminds Arjuna of his dharma or religious duty, which is closely related to his caste. Similarly, a Hindu practitioner is meant to avoid violent behaviour in order to avoid negative karma. A good example of following the principle of Ahimsa is vegetarianism. Animal slaughter and eating meat is seen to accrue negative karma. However, it is important to note that not all Hindu's are vegetarians; it is common in Hinduism, but not required of all castes.

In modern times, Ahimsa has proved to be an enduring and still relevant philosophy. In India, it was the spiritual inspiration for Mahatma Gandhi's philosophy of satyagraha. This was a political philosophy that urged non-violence and passive resistance. Gandhi's philosophy became the leading method used in the Indian struggle for independence against Britain and has directly inspired other non-violent resistance leaders and movements, such as Martin Luther King and the US civil rights movement.

Despite understandable justifications for violence, Hinduism's central virtue is non-violence. It is directly related to central doctrinal beliefs in Hinduism related to the nature of the individual soul and God. Ahimsa is the moral or ethical code of Hinduism. Despite the presence in the Hindu tradition of justifications for violence, violence is still presented as a last resort and only acceptable within the framework of dharma or religious duty. **[6 marks]**

2. The Vedas, meaning 'knowledge', or 'wisdom' in Sanskrit, are the oldest sacred texts in Hinduism, written in a period between 1500 and 1000 BCE. They are organized in four main books, the Rig Veda, Yajur Veda, Sama Veda and Atharvaveda. Hindus believe that the Vedas were 'heard' by wise men or Rishis in deep meditation and can be considered the revealed or heard word of God. However, despite their age and revealed status, there is much to support the argument that the Vedas are 'irrelevant and inaccessible' to most Hindus. To begin with, the Vedas are seldom read by Hindu practitioners and are meant for a limited audience: Brahmins or twice born Hindus; lower caste Indians and women are forbidden from studying the Vedas.

The Vedas are the earliest and most authoritative of Hinduism's vast collection of sacred texts, classified as Shruti texts or 'heard' texts. Other sacred texts in Hinduism are classified as a Smriti, or 'remembered' texts. Smriti texts are not as authoritative. Despite the authoritative and revealed nature of the Vedas, most Hindu practitioners favour other texts, such as the much-loved epic the Bhagavad Gita, probably the most popularly studied, accessible sacred text in Hinduism, and the Ramayana, or the collection of Hindu mythology related to the many manifestations of the divine in Hinduism as expressed in the Puranas. Hindus interact with these texts in many ways, by reading them but also by experiencing them in musical plays and performances, and in modern times as TV soap operas which bring the stories of the many gods and goddesses of classical Hinduism to people's homes.

The Vedas are inaccessible to most Hindus for several reasons. To begin with, they are written in Sanskrit, an ancient holy language that most modern-day Hindu practitioners do not know, and so they are difficult to access as a result of this linguistic barrier. The majority of Hindu practitioners live in India where thousands of local and vernacular dialects are spoken. The fact that the Vedas are written in Sanskrit does make them inaccessible to most Hindus. Most Hindus have memorized significant mantras used for important life rituals or ceremonies, such as the Hindu marriage ceremony, but they may not have a wider knowledge of the Vedas. It is significant to note that more popular sacred texts such as the Bhagavad Gita are accessible in vernacular languages and are as a result more widely read or experienced.

The nature of the Vedas and the topics of the different sections are also specifically meant as a manual for Brahmins or priests carrying out Vedic rituals. The Vedas provide very specific and important knowledge for Hindu priests and still play an important role in the training of Brahmins or temple priests in India. The Rig Veda provides the words spoken by the main priest, the Yajur Veda includes the ritual formulas for the priest carrying out the ritual, the Sama Veda contains is tunes for the chants used in the ritual, and the Atharvaveda contains formulas for private rituals or cures and spells. However, as a result of the historical development of Hinduism, many of the Vedic rituals described are no longer acceptable today, such as Vedic rituals that include animal sacrifice, so even Brahmin priests remain unfamiliar with much of the knowledge of the Vedas.

In conclusion, the Vedas are a revered and foundational sacred text with arguably limited relevance to most Hindus as a result of their exclusivity to male members of the Brahmin caste with knowledge of the Sanskrit language. The focus in the Vedas on priestly ritual is in stark contrast to the philosophical and searching wisdom literature of the later Upanishads or the more colourful and exciting stories of the gods and goddesses of classical Hinduism. However, despite their seeming irrelevance, knowledge of the Vedas is encouraged as a virtue and as an end in itself. Some Hindus even believe that moksha, or release from samsara, is not possible without Vedic knowledge. **[15 marks]**

3. The Four Noble Truths are considered the most important Buddhist teachings. They are believed to be the subject of Buddha's first teaching to his disciples after meditating under the Bodhi tree and reaching enlightenment. The Four Noble Truths explain the problems of existence and then provide guidance on dealing with these problems. They are at the heart of Buddhist belief and practice and can be considered the most important Buddhist teaching. While they are not the only important Buddhist teachings or beliefs, arguably all other teachings can be linked to the Four Noble Truths. The Buddha said, 'I teach suffering, its origin, cessation and path, that's all I teach.'

The Four Noble Truths outline the main beliefs of Buddhism. The First Noble Truth is the truth of suffering: life is full of suffering, or dukkha. Dukkha is a Pali term; Pali is the language of the Buddhist scripture. The first Noble Truth's focus on suffering has been criticized for presenting a pessimistic view of the world. However, Buddhist practitioners do not see it this way. In the Buddhist worldview, the First Noble Truth is realistic. A more accurate translation of dukkha is feeling unfulfilled or unsatisfied. In the Buddhist sense, there are two main types of suffering: physical as a result of old age, sickness or death, and mental suffering. Even when most things are going well, life can be difficult and unsatisfactory. In the Second Noble Truth, the truth of the origin of suffering, the Buddha claims to have found the root of all suffering. The Second Noble Truth states that the cause of all suffering is tanha: desire or craving for pleasure, material wealth or immortality.

The Third Noble Truth is the truth of the end of suffering. It promises that suffering can end if practitioners can free themselves from their cravings and attachments. The Third Noble Truth hints at the promise of nirvana. If practitioners can extinguish or blow out the fires of greed, delusions and hatred then they can achieve nirvana. The Fourth Noble Truth goes on to explain that the suffering can end if practitioners follow the noble Eightfold Path, also known as the Middle Way. The noble Eightfold Path contains eight steps or actions that are the Buddha's path to the end of suffering.

There are other complex beliefs and doctrines that make up the cannon of Buddhism. Some central beliefs include the beliefs in karma, samsara and nirvana. However, it is important to note that most other important doctrines and beliefs can be linked back to the Four Noble Truths. Buddhism, like other Indian religions, also believes in the cycle of samsara but it is because practitioners do not understand the Four Noble Truths that they are drawn back again into the cycle of rebirth. The five precepts which form the foundation of Buddhist morality are directly linked to the morality section of the Eightfold Path. If people follow the moral precepts, they are following the moral directives of the Fourth Noble Truth, the Eightfold Path.

In conclusion, while the Buddha lived between 566 1–480 BCE, his teachings are still relevant to people today because they focus on the universal and timeless human problem of suffering. The Four Noble Truths form the essence of Buddha's teaching. They present a diagnosis: the cause of suffering is craving; suffering can end; and the path to the end of suffering is by following the Middle Way or the teaching of the Buddha. **[15 marks]**

4. Meditation is an essential practice in Buddhism. It is a part of the noble Eightfold Path, which is the path to enlightenment or nirvana. If a Buddhist practitioner's goal in life is enlightenment, then meditation is an essential spiritual experience. However, when answering this question, it is important to consider the different spiritual obligations made on the Sangha, the monks and nuns of Buddhism, and lay people. Despite the essential nature of meditation, most Buddhists do not actually meditate. Meditation is most important for monks and nuns who are part of the Buddhist Sangha, and who dedicate their lives to meditation.

Meditation is an essential spiritual experience in Buddhism and is an essential element of the Eightfold Path. The Eightfold Path is the path to enlightenment as outlined by the Buddha in the Four Noble Truths. The Eightfold Path includes: right understanding, right thought, right speech, right action, right livelihood, right effort, right mindfulness and right concentration (Samadhi). The Eightfold Path is sometimes organized under three main themes, ethics, meditation and wisdom. In order to achieve the wisdom of right understanding and right thought, we need to use the mental discipline and practice of right effort, right mindfulness and right concentration. The importance of meditation in Buddhism is reflected in the significant diversity of methods and techniques developed in the different schools of Buddhism.

In Theravada Buddhism, also known as 'the way of the elders', most prevalent in Sri Lanka, Laos, Cambodia, Vietnam and Myanmar, there is strong emphasis on self-liberation and the use of meditation and concentration to achieve this. The ideal state is for a practitioner to join the Sangha. In Theravada Buddhism, Sangha refers to the monks and nuns who have chosen monastic life and detachment in order to achieve liberation. Meditation in Theravada Buddhism is the main tool to liberation, escpecially for the Sangh.

The focus of the teaching of meditation here is for monks, although lay people are encouraged to have right view. Lay people support the Sangha, who spend their time in meditation. In modern times, reforms within Buddhism have tried to focus more attention on the laity. Lay people have traditionally held a diminished role. Buddhist reform movements have encouraged meditation for lay people. The spread of Buddhism in the western world has also expanded the definition of the Sangha and has opened meditation up to smaller Buddhist lay communities. Meditation has even become a popular focus in a secular sense.

In conclusion, it is important to understand that the Buddha targeted his teachings at those who could detach from the material world, the Sangha. In most cases there is no expectation that a lay person should meditate. However, historically, particularly in Theravada Buddhism, the laity have played a supportive role in terms of religious experience. In modern times, there are reform movements focused on increasing the role of meditation for lay people. **[15 marks]**

5. The Guru Granth Sahib, also known as the Adi Granth, is without a doubt the most important Sikh sacred text, as it holds the position of a living guru and represents the highest spiritual authority in Sikhism. The Guru Granth Sahib was originally collected by the fifth guru in 1604 but the authorized version used today was prepared by the tenth guru, Guru Gobind Singh, in 1705. The scriptures include the works of the first five Sikh gurus (religious leaders or teachers) along with the works of the tenth guru's father. Towards the end of his life, Guru Gobind Singh declared the book to be his living

successor. This ended the line of human gurus and the Guru Granth Sahib was declared the living and eternal Guru. The Guru Granth Sahib is held as the living word of God and it is essential in Sikh worship and ritual. There are other important Sikh sacred texts, but none enjoys the same status and reverence as the Guru Granth Sahib.

The Guru Granth Sahib outlines the religious, ethical and ceremonial life of a Sikh individual and community. It is 1430 pages long. It contains approximately 6000 hymns and prayers and is held in great reverence by Sikhs. The Guru Granth Sahib contains the most important teachings of the Sikh religion and is considered the 'living word of God'. Sikhs believe that the same spirit that inhabited the ten human gurus was transferred to the Guru Granth Sahib. As a result, it is treated with much reverence and great care is taken with its handling. It is divided into three sections and is organized according to musical notes or ragas. The first hymn in the book is the Mul Mantra, which declares that God is truth, and is considered the central statement of belief in Sikhism. The hymns and prayers in the Guru Granth Sahib describe and praise God and provide the moral and ethical guidance of the Sikh faith. Sikhs even consider the script the Guru Granth Sahib was written in to be sacred. It is written in Gurmukhi or the 'script of the Gurmukhi'. A Gurmukhi is a pious Sikh.

In Sikh Temples (Gurdwaras), the Guru Granth Sahib is the focus of worship. The Guru Granth Sahib plays a central role in Sikh worship and rituals. Prayers and hymns from the scriptures are sung in worship. Every day, a random daily hymn is sung, and whatever verse is read is considered the to be the guru's teaching or Hukam for the day. Sikh temples will post the hymn of the day and share it with their local community and in today's internet age Sikhs can access an individual random daily reading online. However, the central Sikh Gurdwara in Amritsar also shares its daily hymn online for the entire global Sikh community to share in collective reflection on their daily teaching. The Guru Granth Sahib acts as a Sikh practitioner's personal guide; Sikhs should read from it and reflect on its teachings to be on the path to truth or Kartar.

There are other important and revered sacred texts in Sikhism, but there is no equivalent to the Guru Granth Sahib in terms of sacredness and authority of revelation. The Dasam Granth is one such example. This was once thought to be the writings of Guru Gobind Singh and was therefore considered part of the Guru Granth Sahib, but modern Sikh scholars believe large parts of it to be the work of his disciples and followers and have called its authenticity into question. The Guru Granth Sahib does not hold the status of a living guru; it is seen as being of human origin and that is the major distinction between the Guru Granth Sahib and other texts. Other important Sikh sacred texts include narratives of the lives of the gurus, and hagiographic, historical and devotional writings. One such example is the Janam-sakhi, which includes writings on the life of Guru Nanak. These writings are used by Sikhs to illustrate certain teachings, and develop their understanding of their faith, but they are not seen as being of divine revelation.

The Sikhs refer to their religion as Gurmat or the 'way of the guru'. This shows us the important position the ten Sikh gurus occupy, the final embodiment of these gurus being the Guru Granth Sahib, the eternal guru. This is the principal Sikh sacred text and is seen as the 'living word of God'. There are other important and venerated texts in Sikhism, but the Guru Granth Sahib is more than just a sacred text: it is the living guide to the Sikh religion. By following the teaching of the Guru Granth Sahib, Sikhs believe they are on the path to truth. **[15 marks]**

6. 'All beings and creatures are His, He belongs to all,' proclaims the Guru Granth Sahib. Equality is a central concept in Sikhism and Sikhs are meant to work towards establishing social justice and minimizing poverty. Guru Nanak taught that all people were equal. 'The pious see all as one, with divine light in each heart.' Sikh practitioners believe in the equality of humanity, regardless of race, gender or religious belief. Sikhs stand for justice and equality for all. However, despite the centrality of equality in Sikh religious belief, this is not always applied. There is evidence of social, economic and gender discrimination in Sikh communities, as a result of social and cultural influences. Sikhism is very clear on its rejection and condemnation of all forms of inequality.

The ideal society according to Sikhism is one in which all races and religions can live and worship God in equality. Guru Nanak taught that 'The lowest of the low born, the utmost and very low, Nanak is with those people! What need have I for the high? Wherever the low receive care, surely there are Your blessings.' This indicates a deep concern with improving society and minimizing social and economic injustice. Sangat (worshipping together) and pangat (eating together in langar or community kitchens) and meals for all, help to institutionalize the idea of equality in religious belief and practice. However, in practice, both historically and in contemporary times, social and cultural influences sometimes mean these teachings of equality are not always applied. There is evidence of historical divisions between rural farmer and urban mercantile Sikh communities, which have continued as a result of the social and economic differences between these two communities.

Sikhism does not believe in caste and condemns the practice. It is important to understand that Sikhism emerged in the social context of the Hindu caste system, which divides society into strict social and economic classes. In Sikhism everyone is equal, 'There is not Caste in the hereafter'. The langar or communal kitchen originated as a protest against the caste system. In a langar, everyone sits in a straight line, and eats together, establishing the equal status of all. However, it is important to understand that even though Sikhism condemns the hierarchies of the caste system and teaches equality, Sikhs still belong to castes. The majority belong to the agrarian Jat caste. Much smaller in number but far more powerful are the richer mercantile castes, the Khatri and Arora castes. There is discrimination against Dalit castes, leading Dalit Sikh communities to build their own community Gurdwara. So, despite the teachings of equality, some levels of discrimination do exist and are most clearly seen in terms of marriage, as Sikh practitioners tend to keep within their caste when marrying.

The role of women as outlined in Sikh scripture is equal to the role of men. Sikh practitioners believe that men and women have the same soul and therefore they have equal religious rights. They have equal rights to grow spiritually and should not be excluded from certain prayers or rituals. Sikh gurus condemned female infanticide and sati, or widow burning, and present clear teaching on equality. There is no difference between men and women in terms of Sikh religious initiation, or sangat or worshipping together, and pangat, eating together. In Sikhism, women have just as much right as men to lead religious congregations and perform Kirtan, or congregational singing of hymns. However, these ideals of gender equality sometimes find it difficult to stand up to social and cultural norms. It is interesting to note thought that even though women have an equal vote in the Sikh central religious body, the Shiromani Gurdwara Parbandhak Committee, they make up only a small percentage of the membership of the committee.

Sikhism emerged in a patriarchal society, with social, economic and caste divides. Many of the teachings of Sikhism are a direct reaction to the injustices of the social, economic, gender and caste divides prevailing at that time. The equality of all human beings is a central concept of the religion. We all have an equal chance at liberation. Despite the strength of these teachings, it would be wrong to assume that social, caste and gender inequalities do not exist: they are present in Sikh society as in any other society. **[15 marks]**

7. **Hinduism**

Marriage is seen by many Hindu practitioners as a sacred ceremony that binds a man and a woman together for life. Marriage is not a personal choice but a social and religious duty. The concept of divorce is foreign to Hinduism, however, it is not explicitly forbidden. In India, where most Hindu practitioners live, the civil law code allows for divorce under certain circumstances, but it is very uncommon for religious as well as social and cultural reasons to seek a divorce. The prevailing attitude is that marriage is a social and religious obligation and divorce is not favoured because marriage is seen as a sacred bond, an important life stage that helps a Hindu practitioner achieve their dharma or religious duty. Divorce would break the sacred bond and accrue bad karma.

Marriage is a samskara, or rite of passage in Hinduism. A Hindu marriage is seen as sacred and has its roots in Vedic rituals. The ceremony is witnessed by the Agni, the Hindu god of fire. A wife is seen as a gift from the gods in Hindu marriage. In a Hindu marriage ceremony, the priest first marries the bride to the gods and then presents her to her husband as a gift from the gods. A husband cannot fulfil his religious duties without a wife and so he must value his wife as a gift from the gods, to help him achieve his religious duties. When Hindus get married, Vedic scripture explains

that they become almost one body: 'Her bones become identified with his bones, flesh with flesh, skin with skin' (Vedas). In a Hindu marriage, it is the atman or individual souls that are married and so the relationship is believed to continue for several lifetimes. Each marriage is destined to be, so a divorce would break this sacred connection. Hindu practitioners believe that marriages should be worked at, and the Ramayana and Bhagavad Gita epics also teach that a husband and wife must stay together despite the hardships of life in order to fulfil their religious duties.

Marriage is arguably the most important rite of passage for a Hindu adult, as marriage allows for a Hindu practitioner's entrance into the second life stage or Ashrama, the Grihastha or householder stage. The husband and wife are brought together in sacred union and are meant to support each other in carrying out their religious responsibilities. Marriage allows a man to fulfil the religious duty of performing sacrifices and having sons. It is not just a bond of personal love or one to fulfil sexual desire but is rather a part of a practitioner's religious life and duty. Marriage allows a woman to fulfil her important role as a wife and mother, and having children is seen as a sacred duty. Divorce is seen by many Hindus as bad karma because divorce does not allow the Hindu individual to achieve the goals of the householder stage, thus making it difficult to achieve one's dharma or religious duty.

Most Orthodox Hindu practitioners agree that divorce is unacceptable. However, Hindu religious law and scripture does provide certain conditions under which divorce can take place. The laws of Manu explain that a marriage may be annulled if it is under false pretences or 'If anybody gives away a maiden possessing blemishes without declaring them, the bridegroom may annul that contract with the evil-minded giver.' If the husband or wife do not love each other, this is also grounds for divorce. Alcoholism is also a ground for divorce according to Hindu scripture: 'She who drinks spiritous liquor, is of bad conduct, rebellious, diseased (with leprosy), violent, or wasteful of money, may at any time be superseded by another wife'. In cases of abandonment a wife can also seek to remarry, 'If the husband went abroad for some sacred duty, the wife should wait for him eight years, if he went for acquiring learning or fame six years and if he went for pleasure three years.' [Thereafter she may remarry without incurring any sin or guilt.]

In conclusion, though many orthodox Hindus may view divorce as unacceptable in Hinduism, there is ample evidence that Hindu scripture does allow for divorce under certain circumstances. This is reflected in civil law codes in India today. However, divorce remains undesirable to many Hindu practitioners for cultural, social and religious reasons.

Buddhism

In Buddhism, marriage is not viewed as a sacrament: it is a secular issue in Buddhism. The Buddha did not discuss marriage or divorce in much detail, other than commenting on the difficulties of marriage. Buddhists follow the civil secular legal codes of the countries they reside in. Buddhism has no restrictions on divorce and if the marriage is a real cause of suffering then divorce is encouraged. The focus of Buddhism is on how a practitioner can best lead their life, to eliminate craving or desires and the suffering they bring along, in order to achieve enlightenment. A Buddhist achieves this enlightenment through detachment and if they join the sangha this is done with a vow of celibacy. Marriage is not part of an individual's path to enlightenment, so divorce is acceptable in Buddhism.

Buddhism focuses on detachment from human desires in this world in order to achieve enlightenment. However, not all Buddhist practitioners aim to achieve this enlightenment in their current lifetime. In Buddhism, marriage is for lay people and is an entirely personal issue. Marriage in Buddhism is not viewed as a sacred sacrament, as unlike in Hinduism or Christianity. Some critics of Buddhism present it as being against marriage, with its focus on detachment and the monastic orders, but that seems a misunderstanding. The Buddha said, 'If a man can find a suitable and understanding wife and a woman can find a suitable and understanding husband, both are fortunate indeed.' Buddhist practitioners hope that marriages are happy and can support an individual's spiritual awakening. The Buddha also commented on the roles and responsibilities that promote harmony between men and women and gave much advice to married couples. Buddhism encourages husbands to be faithful to their wives, and not to seek sensual pleasure with other women. In this way it recognizes the importance of marriage and specifically the importance of a harmonious marriage.

Divorce is not commented on by Buddhist scripture in much detail, clearly it is viewed as a secular issue. However, there is no condemnation of divorce. If a marriage is not harmonious and does not help one achieve happiness, then ending it is desirable. A divorce can be seen as an act of compassion, which is an important behaviour in Buddhism. If a Buddhist couple does choose to divorce, they are encouraged to limit the suffering of those involved, especially if there are children involved, and to carry out the divorce in as harmonious a way as possible. Choosing to remarry is not frowned upon but rather is seen as an opportunity for happiness and the elimination of suffering.

In conclusion, marriage and divorce are secular issues in Buddhism. Since marriage is not seen as a religious duty or sacrament, there are no objections to ending a marriage. The possibility of achieving individual enlightenment is more of a concern to Buddhism. If a marriage is unhappy and prevents individuals from achieving enlightenment, then its end is a positive event. Buddhism is about achieving self-understanding, so if an unhappy marriage is preventing that then divorce is a desirable end.

Sikhism

Sikh marriage is a sacrament and a sacred rite. A marriage in Sikhism is meant to be a permanent event and there is no provision for divorce. In a Sikh marriage ceremony, a Sikh husband and wife promise in front of the Guru Granth Sahib to love and stay together for life, helping each other on their spiritual path. Marriage is the ideal status in Sikhism. Sikhs are encouraged to marry and be faithful to their spouses: 'Be faithful to your 'one wife', see others as your daughters and sisters.' Women 'must be faithful to one husband and see others as your sons and brothers.' There is no religious ceremony for divorce, and Sikh scripture states that no Sikh man can remarry if his first wife is still alive.

Marriage is an obligation in Sikhism. Marriage in Sikhism is not about gratifying sexual desires but is rather about saving an individual from committing sexual sins. The purpose of marriage in Sikhism is not simply for procreation. Marriage is a sacred promise made before God and should not be looked upon lightly; a decision to end a marriage can only be given in very extreme circumstances. The Sikh marriage ceremony, or Anand Karaj, translates as blissful event, giving us an indication of the importance of marriage in Sikhism. Marriage is not only the bringing together of two individuals in mind, body and soul, but also the bringing together of their families.

Marriages and divorces are not really considered a personal matter in Sikhism; traditionally Sikh marriages are arranged, in the sense that the families of the bride and groom try to arrange the most suitable marriage. This is sometimes misunderstood in the western world as forcing the couple into marriage. An arranged marriage takes into consideration the wishes of the couple to make the most suitable marriage, one based on love and respect. Similarly, ending a marriage in Sikhism is not viewed as a personal matter. If a couple experience difficulties, the Sikh community (sangat) will intervene to resolve any differences and help the couple. In many Sikh communities, pressure is put on the couple to resolve or work through their differences rather than seek a civil divorce. However, in extreme cases where it proves impossible to reconcile the couple, permission to remarry can be given.

Divorce is seen as a taboo by many Sikhs. There is no religious ceremony for divorce, indicating its status, however, Sikh practitioners seeking a divorce can resort to the civil code of the countries they live in. Divorce is still a social stigma in the Sikh community. This sometimes means a divorced individual, particularly a woman will find it very difficult to get remarried. Families of men seeking marriage partners will not consider a divorced woman, meaning the possibility of remarriage within the Sikh community is difficult. Attitudes are changing and divorce is becoming more acceptable, particularly in Sikh communities around the world, but it remains a social stigma to many. This has led many Sikhs to marry outside of the community.

In conclusion, marriage is seen as permanent and a sacrament. It is a promise made before God and one that couples are encouraged to work hard at keeping in love and faith. Marriage is not just a marriage of individuals but also a marriage of families, and so ending a marriage is complex. Efforts are made to arrange a suitable marriage so that divorce is avoided. As a result of these religious beliefs divorce is still a taboo for Sikhs, though attitudes are changing. **[15 marks]**

Paper 2: Section B

8. The Torah, both written and oral, form the principal Jewish sacred texts. Jews believe the Torah to be eternally true. It is without a doubt the most sacred of Jewish sacred texts. There are 24 books in the Hebrew Bible, divided into three sections, the Torah (Law), Nevi'im (Prophets), and Ketuvim (Books). These three sections are traditionally referred to using the acronym Tanakh. It is written in Hebrew and is believed to be the word of God. It is believed by Orthodox Jews to have been dictated to Moses on Mount Sinai, after the Jewish exodus from Egypt, dating to around 1312 BC. It outlines how Jews should live their lives and is commonly believed to contain 613 commandments. Attitudes to the Torah and thus its importance differ between different Jewish sects. The two main points of contention are the divine origins of the Torah and how strictly Jews should apply the 613 commandments, or the Halakha derived from the mitzvot.

The word Torah means 'law' or 'teaching' and is often used to refer to both the written and oral Torah. The written Torah is the first five books of the Jewish bible: Genesis, Exodus, Leviticus, Numbers, and Deuteronomy. The Torah documents the creation of the universe, the history of the Patriarchs, Abraham, Isaac and Jacob, and the Israelites. It is an important document of Jewish religious history. It is important to note that the term Torah also includes what is referred to as the Oral Torah, which includes interpretations or clarifications of the written Torah made by rabbis and now collected in the Talmud and Midrash. The Oral Torah is traditionally believed to have been revealed to Moses at Mount Sinai and provides clarification on the written Torah. Originally orally transmitted, the Oral Torah was eventually written and compiled around 200 CE in the Mishnah and later in the Gemara, which included new interpretations of Jewish Law developed after the Mishnah. The Mishnah and the Gemara together are referred to as the Talmud.

Reading the written Torah is an important Jewish religious ritual. The Torah is read from widely in Jewish religious ceremonies. The Torah is read on the Shabbat Saturday morning in 52 weekly sections called a Sidra, that allow the reading of the entire Pentateuch over the course of the year. Simchat Torah is an annual holiday celebrating the completion of the annual reading. Sections of the Torah are read at important rites of passage such as Bar Mitzvah or Bat Mitzvah ceremonies.

Orthodox Jews believe the Torah is the literal and unchanging laws of God. According to Orthodox Judaism, the Halakha or Jewish Law is the best understanding of the Torah and must be followed. On the other end of the spectrum, Reform Jews view the Torah as a holy but historical document, written by humans and not of divine origin. They consider it a matter of personal choice whether to follow the Halachic obligations or not. Somewhere between the two extremes Conservative Jews believe the Torah to be the Law of God but they are open to the idea that the interpretations of these laws can be developed and interpreted for modern times.

Despite the Torah's paramount position, there are other sources of authority that include the second section of the Hebrew Bible the Nevi'im and the Ketuvim. The Ketuvim is the third section of the Hebrew Bible and includes 12 books in total, comprising poetry, songs and wisdom literature.

The Torah is the central text of Judaism and is traditionally believed to be of divine origin. It plays a central role in Jewish religious rituals and ceremonies. It is the foundation of Jewish religious law or Halakha. Modern Jews disagree about the divinity of the Torah, but they all agree that it provides guidance for a Jews life. **[15 marks]**

9. The Shabbat is considered the fourth of the ten commandments and every week religious Jews around the world observe its traditions and customs. It is a reminder to Jews of their covenant with God and their obligation to follow the commandments. Shabbat is the seventh day of the week and is the Jewish day of rest. The Sabbath is a time to forget about work and the demands of everyday life. The Torah commands Jews to remember the Shabbat and keep it holy. God created the world in six days and rested on the seventh and so should humans. On the Sabbath, observant Jews refrain from work; they rest and spend time with family and in spiritual contemplation. The Sabbath is of great importance in Judaism and is viewed as a joyous and festive holiday. Jews are expected to honour the Sabbath: they will get dressed up and many look forward to Shabbat all week.

The Shabbat also includes many Jewish religious traditions and customs, which help Jews observe the Sabbath. Shabbat begins at sunset on Friday and ends at sunset on Saturday. The Shabbat is a day of rest: no cleaning, cooking or chores are allowed on the Shabbat so there is much preparation for the day beforehand. All preparations need to be completed before sunset on Friday. If possible, many Jews will leave work early on Friday to be home in time to celebrate Shabbat with their families. The Shabbat table is laid and two loaves of bread called challah bread are placed on the table. The baking of challah bread for Sabbath is also considered a mitzvah.

The beginning of Sabbath is marked by the lighting of two candles. According to Jewish tradition, each candle represents a commandment, the commandment to remember the Sabbath and the commandment to observe the Sabbath. The candles are usually lit by the mother of the household. She will then cover her eyes and say a blessing. This is followed by the father of the house filling the Kiddush cup with wine and saying the Kiddush blessing. He then blesses the challah bread and a slice is cut for everyone. Other blessings or prayers may be said. More food is then brought in and the family share the Shabbat meal. Special foods are prepared for the Shabbat meal, as this is a holiday to be enjoyed with good food and family.

On Saturday morning, a Jewish family will go to the synagogue listen to a sermon by a rabbi and readings from the Torah. It is customary to have three festive meals during Shabbat: the Friday dinner that marks the beginning of Shabbat is followed by Shabbat lunch on Saturday and a meal eaten late on Shabbat afternoon. Jews are encouraged to enjoy Shabbat, to eat well and enjoy the company of their family. When three stars appear in the sky on Saturday evening it marks the end of Sabbath. The end of Sabbath is also marked by a ceremony called the Havdalah, a farewell to Shabbat ceremony. The Havdalah blessing is recited over a cup of wine, fragrant spices are burned, to remind Jews of the sweetness of the Shabbat, and a braided candle is burned, the candle representing the strength of the Jewish people and their covenant with God.

Jews differ in how strictly they observe the Shabbat. Orthodox and conservative Jews strictly follow the no work commandment, so much so that in many cases switching on lights, using electricity, or driving a car is prohibited. Many modern-day technologies such as timers on light switches have been developed to get around these problems. Reform or reconstructionist Jews believe it is the individual Jews' choice whether to observe Shabbat prohibitions or not.

For many, the Shabbat is a much looked forward to event at the end of each week, a chance to forget the world of work and worldly demands. Jews are encouraged to read, study, and discuss the Torah, attend a synagogue and socialize with their families on Shabbat. The fact that Shabbat occurs every week is part of its importance, as most other Jewish festivals are annual events. **[15 marks]**

10. A baptism or christening is an essential sacrament in Christianity and marks an individual's entry into the faith. The types and rituals of baptism vary amongst different churches; however, they share the use of water, and the use of the Trinity invocation, 'I baptize you in the name of the Father, the Son and the Holy Spirit.' A sacrament is a Christian religious rite in which it is believed that sacred powers are transmitted through material objects, in the case of baptism, through water. Water is either poured or sprinkled over the head of the person being baptized, or the rite can sometimes involve immersion in water. In most churches, baptism is seen as a requirement for salvation. It cleanses away sins and confers grace. 'But you were washed, you were sanctified, you were justified in the name of the Lord Jesus Christ and by the Spirit of our God.' Baptism rituals vary among different denominations, as do opinions on the significance of the rite and when it should occur.

The bible and Jesus himself call for people to be baptized, 'Therefore, go and make disciples of all nations, baptizing them in the name of the Father and of the Son and of the Holy Spirit', and makes a strong connection between baptism and salvation, 'Anyone who believes and is baptized will be saved'. However, the bible does not outline any specific rituals or comment on the significance of baptism. As a result, many different approaches to baptism have developed along with disagreements on the form and significance. In eastern Orthodox churches, for example, infant baptism involves full immersion three times in water. However, in Catholic baptism, the practice is to pour holy water over the infant's head.

There is some disagreement over when a person should be baptized. Roman Catholics, Anglicans and Orthodox Christians practice infant baptism. Presbyterians believe that infants should be baptized. The infant has water poured or sprinkled over their head or is fully immersed in water as part of the baptism ritual, the water symbolically washing away original sin and welcoming the child into the church. However, other Christians, such as the Baptists and most evangelical churches, disagree and argue that only adults, who are conscious of their decision and can repent for their sins, should be baptized. They believe that the experience requires maturity in order to understand its significance, and feel that they are following the example of the baptism of Jesus Christ. Other beliefs about baptism include the belief that it is a sacrament that confers grace. Most Christians believe that baptism is necessary for salvation and deliverance.

In conclusion, there is much agreement that baptism signifies the entrance of an individual to the church, and it is generally believed to be a requirement for salvation. The rituals involved in a baptism ritual very from church to church and culture to culture. The main disagreement seems to be around the issue of when a practitioner or infant should be baptized. Most Christian churches baptize infants but a minority, such as evangelical Christians, insist on adult baptism. They believe baptism must be a conscious choice made by an adult for it to be meaningful. **[15 marks]**

11. Pacifism is a rejection of violence, particularly the use of violence to resolve conflicts. A pacifist, for example, rejects war and does not support the idea of violent resistance. Though Christianity and Christian scriptures do teach peace and love for other human beings, it is difficult to describe Christianity as a pacifistic religion since there are justifications for the use of violence, in certain circumstances, such as preventing injustice or defending the religion. However, many Christians believe that Jesus was a pacifist and that any form of violence is incompatible with their Christian faith.

The roots of Christian pacifism can be found in the Old Testament, which contains many teachings promoting peace. The ten commandments command 'thou shalt not kill' and command practitioners to 'Love thy neighbour'. However, the Old Testament is also full of examples of violence and warfare, with examples of God taking vengeance on his enemies. 'I will destine you to the sword, and all of you shall bow down to the slaughter, because when I called you did not answer, when I spoke, you did not listen.' God is also seen in the Old Testament fighting alongside the Israelites in what can be described as a righteous war. This seems to contradict the belief that Christianity is a pacifistic religion as it also seems to support the use of violence under certain circumstances.

The New Testament is strongly associated with the pacifism of Jesus. Many Christians believe the New Testament commands pacifism. The Sermon on the Mount is probably the most common example used to point to the pacifism of Christianity. In the sermon Jesus says, 'You have heard that it was said, you should love your neighbour and hate your enemy. But I say to you, love your enemies and pray for those who persecute you.' Jesus also goes on to say Christians must turn the other cheek when attacked and 'Blessed are the peacemakers.' This evidence supports the idea that there is a pacifist message contained in Jesus' teachings.

Early Christian theologians, such as St. Augustine of Hippo, argued that sometimes we are forced to use violence to fight evil. St. Augustine argued that the pacifism of Jesus is only possible in what he called 'the city of God' but was not applicable in 'city of man'. He argued that war was acceptable if it was a just war. This was an attempt to limit war by setting some restrictions on violent conflict. In the 13th century, St. Thomas Aquinas argued that war and violent conflict can at times be justified. He outlined three conditions for the use of violence. He argued that war was justified if it was approved by the proper authority, if it was a just war, and finally if its aim was to reduce suffering and evil. If these conditions are met then, according to Aquinas, war is justified and morally sanctioned.

Despite the presence of justifications for violence, many Christian practitioners believe Christianity to command pacifism. In fact, many Christian denominations, including the Quakers and Mennonites, consider peace and pacifism a central doctrine of Christianity. Other denominations such as Calvinists, Lutherans and the Anglican Church acknowledge pacifism and reject the use of war as incompatible with Christianity. In conclusion, there are strong teachings that promote peace, love and non-violence in Christianity, however, there are also equally valid justifications for the use of violence that been used to morally sanction war, so Christianity follows a form of conditional pacifism. Pacifism is the ideal state but realistically violence is sometimes necessary. **[15 marks]**

12. In Islam there are two principal sacred texts. The first and most important is the Qur'an. The Qur'an is believed by Muslims to be the spoken verbatim word of God, as revealed to his messenger, the prophet Muhammad (PBUH), through the Angel Gabriel. The Qur'an is incomparable to any other sacred text in Islam and is greatly revered. It was written down in the prophet Muhammad's lifetime and collected in an authorized version not long after his death. Its divine revelation is the basis of its authority. The Hadith, in Arabic meaning speech or report, are the collected traditions of the prophet, sayings ascribed to the prophet Muhammad (PBUH), orally transmitted and then finally collected and organized in the ninth century. The Hadith are the traditions of the prophet Muhammad (PBUH); they do not have a divine nature, and they form a second tier of importance. However, the authorized and accepted versions of the Hadith, such as Sahih Bukhari and Muslim, form the basis of Islamic laws or Sharia, making the Hadith of vital importance. The oral nature of the Hadith and their much later collection has led some Muslim scholars to reject the reliability of the Hadith, but these are in the minority in the Muslim umma.

The Qur'an is the single most authoritative text in Islam. It is believed by Muslims to be the word of God. When a Muslim recites the Qur'an, or more commonly listens to a recitation of the Qur'an, they are listening to God speaking to them. Most Muslims, observant or not, speak commonly about the power the Qur'an has, especially when listened to in recitation. Muslims believe the inimitability or (Ijaz) of the Qur'an to be proof of the truth of their faith. This is the belief that no human speech can match its content and form. The early documentation and collection of the Qur'an means there is much agreement on its reliability. The Qur'an is relatively short, about 400 pages in English translation. It consists of 144 surahs, organized in order of length, the longest surahs are at the beginning and the shortest at the end. Its organization bears no relationship to the chronological order in which the verses were revealed. The Qur'an was revealed over a period of 22 years, between the beginning of the revelation in 609 CE until the death of the prophet Muhammad (PBUH) in 632 CE. The companions of the prophet first committed the verses to memory, but very early on wrote the verses down. By the time the prophet had moved to Medina, he had several secretaries to whom he dictated his revelations. This early documentation means there is little disagreement on the accuracy of the verses.

The Hadith or traditions of the prophet Muhammad (PBUH) are the second most important source of Islamic teachings. The Hadith are the collections of sayings by the prophet Muhammad (PBUH), committed to memory by his companions and eventually written down and documented. The Hadiths are an illuminating accompaniment to the Qur'an. The Hadiths illustrates many of the historical or contextual background to the revelations and other events in the prophet's lifetime. For examples the Hadiths, tell us that the earliest revelations were received in a state of trance and caused the prophet to cry out and shiver uncontrollably. The Hadiths also comment on ethical or religious obligations, on issues of daily life, and provide clarifications on religious teachings. The Qur'an does not go into much detail on certain aspects of Islamic law, and in many cases the Hadiths do, or provide examples that can be used to measure the correct course of action. The Shia include the Hadith of all the Ahl al-Bayt in their collections of Hadith and include both the Hadith of the prophet but also those of Ali bin Abi Taleb and his sons.

Though some in the Muslim community have questioned the reliability of the Hadith, it is also important to comment on the methods used by those who collected the Hadith to assure reliability. Early Muslim scholars used systems of isnads (chains of authorities) to support the reliability of their Hadith. The Hadith will begin with an attestation that this person said the prophet said something; the longer the chain of isnads, the less reliable the Hadith. Hadith are categorized as ṣaḥīḥ (correct), ḍaīf (weak), or mawḍū (fabricated). The Qur'an teaches Muslims that they must 'Obey God, and obey His Messenger.' This helps clarify the importance of the Hadith and the basis of their authority. The prophet Muhammad (PBUH) is a role model to all Muslims and practitioners aspire to be like the Prophet in words and actions. 'Ye have indeed in the Messenger of Allah the best example for any whose hope is in Allah and the Final Day, who always remember Allah.'

In conclusion, the Qur'an and Hadith are the principal sacred texts of Islam. However, one is of divine origin and the other of human origin. Because of the nature of the Qur'an and its ability to be interpreted in different ways, the Hadith is sometimes used to explain the Qur'an and also forms the basis of much of the Sharia. However, the Qur'an is the most authoritative as it is considered the word of God. **[15 marks]**

13. Al-Fatiha is the first surah or chapter of the Qur'an. In Arabic, Al-Fatiha means the opener or the opening, a reference to the fact that it is the first chapter of the Qur'an, but it also plays an opening role in other aspects of a Muslim's life, most significantly daily ritual prayer, or Salat. However, it has also been described as the surah that helps open a believer's heart to the messages of the Qur'an and so it is, literally and spiritually, the opener. It has been described by many as containing a succinct synthesis of the central beliefs of the faith. The prophet Muhammad (PBUH) referred to this surah as, 'Umm Al Kitab' or the mother of the book, which gives a clear indication of its importance and status in Islam.

The surah contains seven ayahs or verses and 25 Arabic words. The first verse begins with the familiar, 'In the name of God, the compassionate, the merciful'. In the second verse 'All Praise belongs to God, Lord of the Worlds', we must praise God, who is the Lord of both this world, Al Dunia, and the next world to come, Al-Akhira. Thus, very early on in the first surah in the Qur'an, we are introduced to a basic understanding that there is a world to come, Al-Akhira. God is described again and praised in the third verse as 'The Merciful, the Compassionate'. This is a repetition of the previously mentioned characteristic of God in the first verse. In the fourth, God is described as the 'Master of the Day of Judgment.' In this verse, we are introduced to another central concept in Islam, the day of judgement.

The fifth verse declares, 'It is You we worship; it is You we ask for help.' God is the object of worship in Islam, Muslims must remember God in all that they do; they must ask God for guidance, for forgiveness and supplication. They must praise God and remember his divine qualities. God is compassionate and merciful, but God is also the master of the day of judgement and so in verse six practitioners must ask God to 'Guide us on the Straight Path'. The straight path or Sirat Al-Mustaqeem is a central idea in Islam. Muslims must keep on straight path as outlined by the Qur'an and the prophet Muhammad (PBUH). Verse seven mentions the 'Path of those You have blessed, not of those who have evoked [Your] anger or of those who are astray.' The devil may tempt Muslims away from the straight path, but they must keep their minds focused on God. So, there is an acknowledgement of human effort in attaining the straight path but also the idea that God will bless certain people along this path or Sirat al Mustaqeem.

Al-Fatiha plays an important role in Muslim daily ritual prayer. It is the first prayer used in Muslim prayer when starting a new prayer cycle, or raka'ah. The prophet said, 'Whoever does not recite Al-Fatiha in his prayer, his prayer is invalid.' An observant Muslim carrying out Salat or prayer five times a day will repeat the Fatiha around 17 times a day. It is also of great importance because the Hadith suggests it holds a special position in the Qur'an. The prophet referred to the Fatiha as 'The mother of the Qur'an is the seven oft-repeated verses (Al-Mathaini) and is the Great Qur'an [Sahih Al Bukhari].'

In conclusion, Al-Fatiha is the most important surah of the Qur'an if we consider its frequency of daily use, particularly in daily prayer. It outlines the main beliefs of Islam, the belief in the one true God, who is the Lord of the worlds. The Al-Fatiha explains that there is a judgement day and divine recompence. In the Al-Fatiha, a practitioner is praising God and seeking god's blessing in helping them stay on God's path. The greatest proof of the importance of these verses is in the Qur'an itself, 'And We have bestowed upon you [Muhammad] the seven oft-repeated (verses) and the great Qur'an'. The mention of the Al-Fatiha here as the seven repeated verses is a clear indication of its special status. **[15 marks]**

14. **Judaism**

There is a diversity of opinion on abortion in Judaism. There are both strict and more lenient opinions on abortion. Most Jews would agree that they do not support abortion without a valid reason. Abortion contradicts God's commands to populate the earth. Many orthodox denominations see abortion as equal to homicide and only allow abortion in cases where there is evidence the mother's life is at risk. However, most non-orthodox denominations are more lenient and consider more widely the issues of the mother's well-being. According to the Pew Research Centre, 83% of American Jews are pro-choice. Jewish sacred texts reveal a nuanced attitude to abortion and have been interpreted differently. There is agreement, for example, that abortion is allowed if there is a threat to a women's life, the only problem is that there is disagreement over what constitutes a threat: loss of life or psychological harm.

Many Jewish sacred texts agree that a person does not have full personhood until birth. In Exodus Ch. 21 verses 22–23, 'If people are fighting and hit a pregnant woman and she gives birth prematurely but there is no serious injury, the offender must be fined whatever the woman's husband demands and the court allows. But if there is serious injury, you are to take a life for a life.' In this case, men who harm a pregnant woman, leading to a miscarriage, are only fined. This has been interpreted by rabbis to mean that a foetus is not a person yet, since the miscarriage only led to a fine while murder would have led to more severe punishment.

In the Mishnah, if the foetus is threatening the mother's life then it can be destroyed. 'If a woman is having trouble giving birth, they cut up the child in her womb and bring it forth limb by limb, because her life comes before the life of [the child]' but the moment it leaves the birth canal, then all efforts must be made to save both lives. This highlights the belief that a person is not a person until birth, and this interpretation is used to justify abortion. The Talmud supports this argument and claims the foetus does not have a soul or Nefesh until birth. According to halakha, a foetus is part of the mother's body and not a separate living entity till birth. Jewish Law is more lenient towards abortion within the first 40 days, since Jewish scripture states that for the first 40 days the foetus is not a human being.

Orthodox Jews generally are against abortion. They will allow an abortion only if the mother's life is in danger. Similarly, conservative Jews also only permit abortions if the mother's life is in danger, or if there is risk of emotional or psychological harm to the mother. Abortion is also permitted if the foetus is liable to have a life-threatening disability. Reform Judaism permits abortion if the women's life is at risk, but also in cases of rape, or if the foetus has genetic defects, leading to illness or deformities. Reform Judaism argues that this decision is for the woman to make. Reform Judaism has been quite vocal in supporting legal abortions and reproductive rights in the US. In Israel today, abortion is legal under certain circumstances. There is a termination committee that investigates requests for abortions, granting almost all requests, which is paid for by state funds.

In conclusion, abortion is undesirable in Judaism because Judaism values the sanctity of human life. However, Judaism is not strictly anti-abortion. Abortions are allowed in the first 40 days of pregnancy as it is believed the soul is not yet in the foetus. Abortion is also permissible if the mother's life is at risk. Different Jewish groups have diverse viewpoints ranging from the strict to the more lenient.

Christianity

In contemporary Christianity there are different views on abortion. Pro-life denominations argue that all human life, including an embryo or foetus, is sacred and all efforts should be made to preserve that life. Other Christian denominations can be described as pro-choice, in that they support the right of a woman to access a legal abortion. Some Christian denominations condemn all types of abortion as morally wrong, whereas others argue that abortion is acceptable under certain circumstances. The Christian bible does not specifically mention or prohibit abortion, in either the Old or the New Testament, but it does focus on the sanctity of human life and that has been interpreted by many to mean abortion is a sin. There is much debate and argument regarding this issue amongst Christians.

Despite the silence of the sacred texts on abortion, many Christians view abortion as a grave sin. Catholic practitioners for example, are particularly stringent in their attitude to abortion, family planning and contraceptives. They are supported in this by several evangelical or protestant groups. According to the Catholic Church, human life begins at conception. The sixth commandment states 'thou shalt not kill' and this is used to support anti-abortion arguments. According to Canon 1398, anyone who has successfully had an abortion is automatically excommunicated. Excommunication is the harshest punishment at the church's disposal, as it means the excommunicated individual can no longer share in communion, or the spiritual benefits of being part of a Christian community.

The Catholic Church is against all forms of abortion that would lead to the destruction of a foetus or embryo, unless the mother's life is in grave danger. Pope John Paul II said in 1995, 'No circumstances, no purpose, no law whatsoever can make licit an act which is intrinsically illicit.' The only exception made by the Catholic Church is if the mother's life is in danger. The Eastern Orthodox Church shares similar beliefs to those of practising Catholics, in that they agree that a human life begins at conception and therefore abortion is unacceptable. Similarly, the Eastern Orthodox Church makes an exception if the mother's life is in danger, and she already has children, in this case, as long as she confesses her sin and carries out the penance assigned to her by the priest, she will not be excommunicated.

Protestants display a wide range of views on abortion. Conservative Protestants or evangelical Christians tend to be anti-abortion, whereas mainstream Protestant denominations tend to be to support abortion rights. Evangelical Protestants tend to be strongly against abortion and have worked to increase restrictions on legal abortions. In the United States, for example, the recent 2019 Alabama law, called the Human Life Protection Act, makes abortion a felony and only offers two exceptions: grave risk to the mother, or a lethal foetal anomaly. However, other mainstream and less fundamentalist Protestant denominations argue strongly that this is an issue of individual choice, and seek to limit government restrictions on abortion.

In conclusion, Christians believe in the sanctity of human life. All human life is sacred, and all efforts should be made to protect and respect human life. Even amongst groups who are pro-choice and who support the right of women to make their own decision, abortion is still seen as morally wrong. Most Christians agree that abortion should not be used as a form of family planning or contraception but one reverted to in extreme cases. Despite the official positions of many Christian denominations and churches, Christian individuals in many cases can have very different beliefs than their church on the issue of abortion.

Islam

Islam holds the sanctity of life as most important and so views abortion as morally wrong, but also concedes there are certain circumstances in which abortion can be allowed, for example, Muslim practitioners universally agree that the life of the mother takes precedence over the life of the foetus and so if the mother's life is at risk, abortion is permissible. They agree to this based on the idea of greater evil: it would be of greater evil for the mother to die, as she is the source of life and the foetus is only potential life. Islamic schools of Sharia tend to differ on the details rather than the big picture. Major disagreements relate to when the abortion is permissible and reasons for abortion other than the mother's life being at risk.

The Qur'an does not directly mention the issue of abortion and so Muslim practitioners' views on abortion are shaped by Hadith, and the opinions of Muslim scholars. According to Hadith the punishment for abortion after the foetus becomes a soul is hell. However, Islam places sanctify of life in high regard, 'Whosoever has spared the life of a soul, it is as though he has spared the life of all people. Whosoever has killed a soul, it is as though he has murdered all of mankind.' The Qur'an also says, 'Kill not your offspring for fear of poverty; it is We who provide for them and for you. Surely, killing them is a great sin.' This seems to clearly go against abortion for economic reasons.

All Muslims agree that if the mother's life is in danger, it must take precedence over the life of the foetus. This is because the mother is the source of life. The mother's life is well established and she already has duties and responsibilities. Allowing the mother to die would, in most cases, lead to the death of the foetus, so it is a logical choice to save the mother. However, even Islamic jurists who see abortion as permissible under certain circumstances still see abortion as morally wrong, but to different degrees, depending on the duration of gestation. 'When the sperm enters the ovaries... its removal would be a sin. Aborting it after it grows...would be a graver sin and the graveness of the sin increases very much...after... it acquires human form and faculties.'

Most Muslim scholars permit abortion before the foetus is a soul, under certain circumstances. In Islam, a foetus is considered a human soul four months after conception. Therefore, in general, abortions are not allowed after four months. However, there is disagreement over the exact duration and when abortion becomes forbidden or haram. Some schools allow abortion up to 16 weeks, others only up to 11. Other exceptions to the rule that are followed by some schools of Sharia or civil codes are the physical or emotional health of the mothers, cases of rape or incest, and foetal disability or abnormality. Twelver Shias also agree that abortion is permissible up to four months or 120 days but only if the life of the mother is in danger, otherwise abortion is not permissible. Muslims living in different Muslim countries follow the laws of the country they live in and there is great diversity of opinion on abortion. In 18 out of 42 majority Muslim countries, abortion is illegal, unless the mother's life is in grave danger.

In conclusion, all life is sacred in Islam. Abortion is not desirable as Islam values the sanctity of all life. However, as a result of this belief, Islam allows abortion universally, if the mother's life is at risk, based on the principle of lesser evil. Less harm is done by keeping the mother alive and so it is the reasonable course of action. There are minor differences in interpretation between different schools of Islamic Sharia, mostly revolving around the timing of an abortion and determining when the foetus becomes a soul. There is also some disagreement over the validity of exceptions other than the mother's life being in danger. Various modern-day realities for Muslims living in Muslim majority countries must also be considered.

[15 marks]

Notes

www.ingramcontent.com/pod-product-compliance
Lightning Source LLC
Chambersburg PA
CBHW080755030726
47592CB00009B/2870